boy meets girl

boy meets girl

40 Couples on How and Where They Met the One

Rachel Safier

author of *There Goes the Bride* and *Mr. Right Now*

A **adams**media

Avon, Massachusetts

Published by
Adams Media, an F+W Publications Company
57 Littlefield Street, Avon, MA 02322. U.S.A.
www.adamsmedia.com

ISBN 10:1-59869-556-8
ISBN 13: 978-1-59869-556-4

Printed in the United States of America.

J I H G F E D C B A

Library of Congress Cataloging-in-Publication Data
is available from the publisher.

This publication is designed to provide accurate and authoritative information
with regard to the subject matter covered. It is sold with the understanding that
the publisher is not engaged in rendering legal, accounting, or other professional
advice. If legal advice or other expert assistance is required, the services of a com-
petent professional person should be sought.
—From a *Declaration of Principles* jointly adopted by a Committee of the
American Bar Association and a Committee of Publishers and Associations

Many of the designations used by manufacturers and sellers to distinguish their
product are claimed as trademarks. Where those designations appear in this book
and Adams Media was aware of a trademark claim, the designations have been
printed with initial capital letters.

*This book is available at quantity discounts for bulk purchases.
For information, please call 1-800-289-0963.*

contents

Boy Meets Girl has been a joy thanks to Jennifer Kushnier, Andrea Norville, and the team at Adams Media; my longtime agent Stacey Glick at Dystel & Goderich; and, especially, the women and men who let me into their lives. Thank you:

Amy & Jason	Beth & Bob
Wendy & Paul	Claudia & Mark
Nancy & Dale	Denise & Rich
Beth & Pat	Anna & Bob
Julie & Kevin	Carolyn & Doug
Susie & Andrew	Rebecca & Dave
Bev & Gordie	Bella & Tony
Priscilla & Scott	Julie & Jeff
Sue & Ron	Rebecca & Greg
Rose & Mike	Susan & Ned
Dixie & Bobby	Lindsey & John
Jen & Matt	Kayla & Keith
Deborah & John	Sarah & Ted
Rachel & Rafael	Amy & Dale
Sarah & James	Amy & Mike
Kate & Leonard	Kimberly & Thomas
Amanda & Michael	Serena & John
Maryann & Robert	Jill & Jim
Lauren & Andrew	Daisy & John
Catherine & Lew	

When I count my blessings, I count you twice.

—Irish blessing

preface

*I*n the middle of the table sat a fancy cut-crystal punch-bowl, and Allen leaned forward to help himself. The punch was delicious—red, cold, and so sweet Allen had no idea it was spiked. So he kept ladling. By the time he tore himself away to flirt with Joan—leaning casually against a wall, she was dark-eyed and beautiful—he was absolutely drunk. And funny—very, very funny. Joan was on her way out of the party, but she asked if Allen wanted to meet up with her and some friends at a nearby diner later on. He said yes and took off as soon as she was out of sight.

He made his way over to his brother's apartment nearby and banged on the door. When his brother answered, Allen told him he was drunk and desperately needed some coffee and a shower. Semi-sobered up, he met Joan and her friends at the diner, where he charmed her some more. When the gathering broke up, he escorted Joan home to Lower Manhattan, then hopped a bus to get himself back to Brooklyn. But he passed out in the bus and woke up in the bus yard.

They were married a year later and lived together, very much in love, for thirty-eight years. The story of my parents' meeting has been making me smile my whole life. My late father used to act the tale out while he told it: Eyes wide, he'd mime pouring cup after cup of punch. Getting drunk and listing around the room, then banging on my uncle's door. I was twenty or twenty-one before he ever shared the ending of the tale of that fateful first meeting. And even then, he said he "fell asleep" on the bus. Sure, Dad.

As the years went on and I kept asking to hear the story again, my father—still funny, very, very funny—started to make up new stories. My mother used to follow him, he'd tell us (listening to the tall tale, she protested, "Allen!" only pretending to be aggrieved), and he couldn't shake her. He'd get into the elevator in the morning, and there she'd be. Just traveling up and down, hoping for a glimpse of him. Or he'd tell us that he was much younger than she (also not true). And while he played stickball in the schoolyard, she'd lean against the fence and call out to him: "Come here, little boy!" He actually thought I'd believe she ever said that.

My father's parents met at a party too (though I don't know what mock meetings my grandfather might very well have concocted over the years). She was eighteen and he was twenty-two, and when he took her out on the dance floor, she stepped all over his feet.

"You must be a great cook," he told her. Flattered, she asked why. He retorted, "Because you can't dance." In a yellowed newspaper clipping I uncovered as a twelve-year-old, I read my grandmother's account of falling in love with this wise guy. The newspaper named it the winner in their "How I Met My Husband" contest.

Ah, love. My mom wore all black on her twenty-fifth birthday because she *knew* she was "over the hill." There was a point there when I too turned my back on love, romance, and my One. Going through a broken engagement can do that to you. But when I again started to seek out the "how we met" stories that I've always loved, I knew I was healing. And when I listened to them—these amazing, amusing, shocking stories of how two total strangers met and clicked—anything began to seem possible again. Henry Wadsworth Longfellow wrote that it often feels like we're all just ships that pass in the night. But sometimes we're actually meeting our better halves bobbing out there in the dark sea.

Sure, I could sit at home and close my heart. But I saw that there were literally millions of diverse, amazing stories out there of boys meeting girls. Some people swear it was love at first sight—like actor Andy Garcia, who told *In Style* magazine in 1999 that he met his wife "in a bar in Florida. And I'm proud to say I proposed to her the first night I met her. Probably about the third thing I said was 'Will you marry me?' I was so overwhelmed by her. That was it—I didn't need to look any further."

Then come those lovers who at first meeting couldn't have disliked each other more. Troubled and soulful Kiwi singer Beth Hart told NZGirl, an online magazine based in New

Zealand, "I met Scotty at the beginning of my . . . tour, but we in no way were intimate . . . we didn't even like each other. We just did not get along." It was only after he helped her through rehab that they ran off to Vegas. Triumphantly, she exclaimed, "I haven't been in trouble since!"

Some happily married couples met as kids. Bev and Gordie got "engaged" in the first grade, while other lovers like Denise and Rich, who broke up and made up several times (with Denise getting engaged to someone else at one point) before they got married—took awhile to get it right.

There are those who left their meetings to fate. That might mean turning to a computer for a match—like Nancy, who "had all the criteria of what I wanted, down to the astrological sign," and when she plugged it in, up came Dale. Or it could apply to Robert, who went cruising in his car hoping to find someone wonderful and met Maryann.

From the ocean to online, somehow, boys are meeting girls, souls are lighting up, and another two have found their One. When you stop to think about it, it's a miracle every time.

boy meets girl

chapter 1

finding love online

*B*ack in sixteenth-century England, Helen Morrison placed the first-known "lonely-hearts" ad in her local Manchester paper. The spinster was looking for love but instead found herself committed to a lunatic asylum for a month by the city's mayor. If the same rules applied today, asylums would be a good place to go looking for a spouse. According to a 2005 study reported by ABC News, 17 million U.S. adults have posted online personal ads, and 21 million have browsed them.

I first heard about online dating back in 2000. I was sharing an airport shuttle in San Francisco with a couple who had flown west to attend their daughter's wedding—and to meet her fiancé for the first time. Making small talk, I asked the parents how the bride and groom had found each other. Clearly shocked themselves, they admitted that she had met the man online. I remember looking at the poor couple and thinking, "My God, their daughter is marrying a total stranger." Her parents didn't look too pleased, either. If the mother's thoughts were visible in a cartoon bubble above her head, I'm pretty sure it would have read, "Yes, he very well may be an axe murderer."

But in the years since, Internet dating has not only lost its stigma, it's also proven itself to be a smart way to find a mate. Maybe that's because with a personal ad, we're laying all our cards out on the table right away. "Look," your date-to-be is saying, "I'm in the market for a wife. I'm a Virgo, carnivore, have two cats (allergic to dogs) and I never go to bed before midnight." Getting all that information up front may seem less than romantic, but as the couples in this chapter prove, romance is alive and well on the Internet.

how jason *met* amy

Met online: September 2003

Met in person: October 2003 in Chantilly, Virginia (at the Washington-Dulles Airport). Jason was thirty-two, Amy was thirty.

Married: May 2005

I moved to Washington, D.C., in 2000, and I had enormous trouble dating. Nothing was really clicking. By 2003, I was getting totally depressed, so my uncle convinced me to sign up for Internet dating. I had just started a new job and was working really hard, and soon I was going to start a lot of traveling. But my uncle had read about a new website called eHarmony and he said, "We'll do it together." He sat down and walked me through it. It has a long personality test—you can't just search through profiles right off the bat. We filled it out for me.

At first, the site sent me no matches at all. Then it sent me a few people. And just before I left for a business trip, it sent me Amy. There are five stages to the eHarmony process. First you can ask each other multiple-choice questions, then short-answer questions. It takes you through the deal breakers. After a few weeks, just when Amy and I had gotten to the stage where we could e-mail each other, my company told me on three days notice that I had to go to Uzbekistan for a month. I e-mailed her and said, "Your profile looks fantastic but I'm leaving for Uzbekistan and don't know whether I'll have e-mail there. Can I e-mail you when I get back?" I didn't hear back from her.

I got on a plane and thirty hours later arrived in Tashkent. Sure enough, there was e-mail. When I got to the hotel and checked in, I found she had e-mailed me back: "Absolutely, but I lived on the Uzbekistan border for two years with the Peace Corps and I can tell you what to go see." She e-mailed me every day for a week, guiding me around. I took her advice and wrote her back often. It was the nicest way to start.

As the weeks progressed, our e-mails got longer and longer. They were less and less about work and the trip. By the end, they were three pages long and totally romantic. One of her best friends worked for my company. I had one of my friends send her friend a reference so she could tell Amy I was a normal guy.

While we were writing, I thought, "I almost don't want to believe how well this is going." The Jewish New Year came and went and we didn't say anything about the holiday. So I wrote to her, "I'm Jewish, is that going to be a problem?" And she wrote back, "For the first time in my life at a family reunion when I'm asked if I have a Jewish boyfriend I'll be able to say yes."

I was in Uzbekistan for about four weeks. After that, I had to go to Sri Lanka for a week and a half before I could go home. During this time we were sending each other long e-mails every day. When I was just about to leave Sri Lanka, she wrote, "I am having crazy thoughts, maybe I should pick you up at the airport." And I wrote back, "If you pick me up at the airport you are going to get the deepest, longest kiss of your life."

My flight home from Sri Lanka was a nightmare. Anything that could go wrong did. The airline lost my luggage, the flight was delayed, and there was a terror incident on the Zurich-to-Frankfurt leg. When I finally landed in Dulles, I smelled bad, and Amy had been waiting for me for two hours. After I finally finished the whole lost-luggage procedure, I walked out to find her standing there. I dropped my hand baggage right there, and before she could speak we kissed in the middle of the airport.

advice for others
look for emotional security.

What first attracted me to Amy was that I could tell her how much I really liked her and it didn't put her off. There were a whole bunch of superficial omens, like the fact that we had the same favorite book, *The Razor's Edge,* which is fairly obscure. But the thing that really told me there was potential was the fact that she just seemed so emotionally open to being in love. I could get excited about our future, and she wasn't afraid of liking me or herself. I could be totally idealistic and romantic. It's great to fall in love in letters. We both could express a lot of idealism.

how wendy *met* paul

Met online: June 1999

Met in person: July 1999 in Las Vegas, Nevada. Wendy was thirty and Paul was thirty-six.

Married: October 1999

Living in Las Vegas, I seemed only to meet men who were just in town for the weekend. Every guy I liked was just in Vegas to party with friends for a few days before returning to a girlfriend back home. Frustrated, I talked to my mom about online dating. She tried to discourage me from doing it (though she denies that now). Though she had met several men that way, she was worried about my safety.

My friends were also reluctant to use Internet dating services because of the stigma. It does seem kind of desperate to place a personal ad online. I used to read the personal ads when I was a kid, and I always thought it was weird that anyone could find anyone else based on such little information. My mom urged me to find more traditional ways to meet men, but I went ahead and posted my profile on Yahoo.

I created an online account that was true except for my last name (to ensure my safety). I planned to e-mail guys for a while before meeting them, in order to weed out anyone who was too aggressive, needy, or sarcastic.

Along with my profile, I posted a long list of the things I was looking for in a man. Politically active, well read and traveled, no kids, liked the outdoors, had done work on childhood issues—the list was extensive. I figured that would scare most men away, but I immediately got over fifty responses. I started reading the e-mails, and most sounded the same: "I work as a bartender, love hiking, blah, blah, blah." I exchanged e-mails several times before meeting any of them, met in a public place, and didn't disclose where I lived or worked.

I met some nice guys and had some good dates. I made sure that I waited a day or two before responding to anyone's calls or e-mails to see who was impatient. I had lots of unstated rules. Anyone who talked about old girlfriends or who tried to kiss me on the first date was out.

One day I got an e-mail response to my ad that immediately snagged my attention—from Paul, an engineer who had two ferrets and did yoga. Hmmm . . . smart, caring, healthy. Potential! We e-mailed back and forth several times, and he sent me a picture of himself without asking for mine. He had the sweetest face I'd ever seen. Okay, I told myself, be patient. The most recent picture I had of myself was after my septoplasty, when I had a huge bandage covering my face from the eyes down. In the picture, I was holding my pet rabbit. I sent him the picture to test his sense of humor. Paul immediately wrote back and said that the rabbit was almost as cute as I was. He then sent a picture of himself at work, wearing a hardhat and safety glasses, standing with some other guys. I asked if they were discussing the project or what to have for lunch. He responded that they were exchanging fashion tips. I was hooked.

After a few weeks, I agreed to meet him. Paul suggested that I come to a pool party at his apartment building that weekend. That seemed pretty geeky, but I liked his enthusiasm, so I agreed. He told me how to find his apartment complex and

tips for getting yourself online

Gail Laguna has plenty of experience with what works (and doesn't) in the online dating world. As spokesperson for Spark Networks—a leading online personals provider whose twenty-seven sites include JDate (for Jewish daters), DeafSinglesConnection, MilitarySinglesConnection and BlackSingles—she offers these tips for standing out online:

Don't just throw something up there. "Take the time to build a profile that will differentiate yours from everyone else's. Everybody likes to laugh, and most people like to go to the movies and walk on the beach. What is your favorite movie? What beach do you want to travel to? What joke makes you laugh every time you hear it? Spend more than twenty minutes cranking out a profile."

Include a photo. "Profiles with photos get up to ten times more responses. And it's not because we're all concerned with meeting the best-looking person—photos show different dimensions of your profile and give a face to the personality. This is especially important in the anonymous online world. Photos establish a certain trust level between people."

Give thought to your username. "Your username should be catchy, sum up who you are, or say something about an interest you have that someone might relate to."

Be open. "Someone may have a lot of typos and not everyone is a great writer, but ultimately you're dating a person, not a profile. And if he's wrong, maybe he's got a friend for you."

Be out there. "Be pro-active. Set aside the time now that you hope to have with that other person later to get online and look through the profiles and communicate with people and those who contacted you."

Decide what really matters. "What is super important? Do you want to raise your kids Jewish? How involved are you with your hobby and how important is it that the other person shares it? Does he have to be five foot ten and not five foot nine?"

that the gate should be open, so just come find him in front of the pool. As I drove up to the complex that day, I could see that the gate was closed, but before I could wonder what to do, I saw Paul sitting outside the gate, waiting for me. He had the foresight to check to make sure that I could get in, and his thoughtfulness struck me. After the pool party, I suggested we go for a drive in his convertible sports car through Red Rock Canyon. We drove along, feeling exuberant and free, and stopped at an overlook to look at the view. I could tell he wanted to kiss me, but he refrained.

Phew! He nearly broke a rule! He took me back to my car and we talked about getting together to go hiking the next weekend.

On that date, he mentioned that he wanted to live overseas. He already had a plan—as a government employee, it was easy to transfer to military bases all over the world. I immediately thought, "I want to go too!" By the end of that hike I knew I had found my soul mate. We went on several road trips over the next few weeks, an activity I knew that was a good test of character. At one point, I backed his convertible over a rock and it scraped the underside of the car. I apologized, but Paul shrugged it off, saying, "It's just a machine." I knew I had found a good man.

One day I tried waxing my legs with a store-bought kit. The wax would not come off, no matter what I tried. I called Paul, who came over and knew chemically what to do. He didn't laugh at me. Instead, he said, "You know I'm going to ask you to marry me soon, don't you?" I loved his straightforwardness. We had only known each other a month, but here was a wonderful guy who had dated lots of women and seen the world. "And yet he's crazy in love with me," I thought. "Is there something about him I'm missing? Does he have some dark secret or past?" I played coy but was falling for him.

His birthday was in a few weeks. I bought him a book of poetry, which was personal but not too personal. As I handed him his present, he kneeled down and presented me with a beautiful tanzanite ring, saying, "The only gift I want is to spend the rest of my life with you."

I accepted his proposal, and we discussed when to have the wedding. Since I'm a counselor, I figured we should wait the customary few months to a year. "Why wait?" he asked, and I knew he was right. Why test things out? We knew we were right for each other, so why let doubts creep into things? His certainty blew me away, and we got married a month later, a total of less than three months after our initial contact.

Seven years later, he continues to be the most thoughtful, caring, incredible husband I could imagine. We have disagreements, but not fights. We agreed early on that there is really nothing in the world worth getting mad at each other over. We live together in Japan, just as we had discussed on our second date, and now we are transferring to Guam, where we have just purchased a beautiful house on a golf course.

Sometimes I'm afraid to tell people about how wonderful he is or how great our life is together. I don't want to brag. I just want people to be happy for us and to know that amazing things are possible. I didn't know it could be like this, but I'm thrilled and grateful that it is, and I wish this happiness for everyone.

advice for others

be clear about what you need.

I think that placing a personal ad online really made me start to think about the character of the person I was looking for, rather than just looking for an attractive man. I made a very specific list of traits that I wanted in a partner. I wanted a man who was politically active, spiritual but not necessarily religious, and not intimidated by the fact that I have a master's degree; who had worked on his childhood issues; and who was a funny, optimistic hiker who appreciated art. Instead of talking about myself in my online ad, I posted the long checklist. Many men were honest in their responses, saying "I don't meet all of your points, but here are the ones that I do." And somehow I found someone who met all the qualities I desired and more!

how **nancy** *met* **dale**

Met online: December 2001

Met in person: April 2002 in Fort Worth, Texas. Nancy was fifty-one and Dale was fifty-two.

Married: December 2002

I love to go dancing, but I don't like to just walk into a club by myself. I don't drink that much, so the bar scene isn't my thing either. And because there aren't a whole lot of singles at my church, I decided to use the Internet.

I wanted to know as much about someone as I could, and of course all the Internet dating services are more detailed now, but at the time Udate had a more comprehensive way to find out about the other person—more in-depth information, what they liked and didn't like, their height and weight, that kind of thing. It's a real advantage, knowing those things about people ahead of time—if they are honest!

I knew all the criteria I wanted, down to astrological sign. When I ran the checklist to see who came up, I came up with only two out of 2,000-something people—and one of them did not physically appeal to me. I would constantly go back in and update my search to see whether it returned anyone else. But Udate said Dale would be my perfect match, and they were right.

One Saturday night I saw Dale was online. I thought, "Well, I'll just say hi," and we started talking. We talked again the next day, and the next day, and so on. I knew from talking

quote/ unquote	"My parents were both eighteen when they met on a train going from King's Cross, London, to Scotland . . . The way my mother told it, a short, dark youth . . . pulled open the compartment door, took a good look around . . . strode over and sat down next to her. When she complained of feeling cold . . . he offered to share his duffel coat with her. From the complacent smirk on my mother's face as she told the story, I gathered that things you don't want to associate with your parents might have gone on under that coat."
	—J. K. Rowling, Interview with National Multiple Sclerosis Society

to him online that we had a lot in common, but it was like he was in love right from the beginning. I said, "You don't even know me yet." He said he just knew that I was it. We were just going to see each other once a month; it's a long way from El Paso, where he lived, to Fort Worth. By the time we got married, we had plenty of frequent flyer miles to go to Vegas.

He flew up to Fort Worth in April for Easter so we could meet in person for the first time. We had talked on the phone and said, "Okay, we'll not make this serious. Let's just see each other every month or every other weekend and meet halfway." But after I finally saw him at Easter we wanted to see each other more than once a month. Even my family knew he was the one for me.

It had only been about three months when we started talking about getting married. He proposed on my birthday in October. We went to a really nice place, and he got down on one knee right there in the middle of the restaurant. He gave me a beautiful ring. Of course I said yes and everyone clapped. His birthday was a few days after mine and we went out to eat at his favorite restaurant. I had already bought his wedding ring and I couldn't wait to show it to him. While we were at dinner I said, "There's something I've got to talk to you about." All the blood drained from his face. Then I said, "I think I have to ask you to marry me, too" and his face lit up. He called it his engagement ring—we got married with our little bands.

We went to Las Vegas and got married in December. He died September 3, 2005, of a massive heart attack. He said that his shoulder and arm were hurting, but then we had been

too much of a good thing?

Not all the people who run internet or newspaper ads think ahead to the day when they won't have to anymore. According to the *Pacific Sun* of Marin County, California, Miki Chavez, "the self-proclaimed 'Queen of the Personals,' . . . has been running an ad in the *Pacific Sun*—and other publications—for over a decade and a half. She touts herself as an 'elegant, charming, former Miss Japan' seeking a 'sociable leader type who values commitment [and] companionship.' Over the years, Miki has received thousands of responses and says that she goes out on a date nearly every night. She has also been married three times and has a son.

"'Finding men is not hard,' says Miki with a laugh. 'There are many out there.'"

doing a lot of work in the yard the day before. He went into the bathroom to take some Motrin, and next thing I thought I heard him getting sick. I found him lying face down on the floor. I turned him over and tried to give him CPR. He was fifty-six, and we had been legally married a little under three years. We never talked about what I would do if something happened to him. I don't know why. He was really in good health. I blamed myself at first; I thought I hadn't given him CPR right. But the doctor said no, he had been too far gone for me to help him. We turned the machines off.

He was my knight in shining armor. He was what I had been looking for my whole life. He was gentle, and he loved me unconditionally. Both of us had been through really, really bad divorces, but he renewed my faith in love. He just took my heart in his hands and gently loved me. I'm not saying there wasn't passion, but it was a warm put-your-arms-around-me-and-everything-will-be-okay kind of love. To find and lose it so quickly was devastating.

Our spiritual beliefs were the same—he was Catholic and he became Methodist, which I am. My father, a Methodist minister, performed his funeral. It was very hard for him, but he said, "Nobody knows him like I did, and I'm supposed to do it." I buried Dale back where he was originally from, in Minnesota, because his mother and sisters and daughters were there.

I made a memorial in my back yard, a memory garden for me here. For him. There are times I can really feel his presence and he's here with me. I always thought a divorce was bad, but it is so much worse to lose somebody you love when you didn't have enough time together. I get angry at God, but I talk to Dale on a regular basis, and we know someday we'll be together again.

advice for others
make memories.

Dale thought of me as his little wild child—I'm really not. We did so many fun things together in our short time together. I got him into riding a motorcycle, and we took motorcycle trips. Every week he played golf with my daddy, who was ninety then. He quit his job and moved up to Fort Worth. We bought a house together. His daughters and his mother said he was happier with me than he had been in all the years of his life. Dale knew I loved him with all my heart. He was happy for the last years of his life, and that's something I always have with me.

how beth *met* pat

Met online: December 2005

Met in person: January 2005 in Boston, Massachusetts. Both Beth and Pat were twenty-nine.

Married: November 2006

I had been on Match.com for about a year, and while I'd met a lot of really nice guys, I never really clicked with any of them. My membership was about to expire, and I decided not to renew it again. I was going to give it one more try and send a few e-mails and winks out, then take some time off. Three days before my membership expired, I saw Pat's picture. Two things stood out—his eyes and his smile.

The picture was in black and white, but I couldn't get over how his eyes sparkled, even on the grainy webcam picture. Sounds cheesy, I know, but I just had to contact him! So I sent him a wink, and never expected to hear from him.

He was online and wrote me an e-mail within minutes. We chatted by e-mail that evening, and then over instant messaging for the next few nights. We were both laughing throughout the IM conversations, and after a few days, we exchanged numbers. We spoke once or twice over the phone, and then we spent New Year's Eve with our respective friends and families.

On New Year's Day, I shot him an e-mail saying that I hoped he was having fun and that I looked forward to talking to him again soon. I didn't know it then, but that's when Pat decided that he really wanted to meet me. He was touched by the fact that I actually thought of him over the holiday.

We went on our first date on January 5th, about a week and a half after we first made contact. We met at a pub in Faneuil Hall in Boston, and then we went to another pub for a casual dinner. I was so nervous that I babbled the whole time—he was so nervous that he barely spoke at all.

We shook hands at the end of the night (no kiss), and he got on the train (the wrong one—he had been living in Massachusetts for just three months and had only been to Boston a handful of times) and thought he'd never see me again. He thought that the date had gone horribly, that he had blown it

when does the average american marry?

We're saying "I do" later and later in life. The median age at first marriage for women has changed over the years:

In 1900, it was 21.9.
In 1950, it fell to 20.3.
In 1998, it rose to 25.1.
In 2006, the median age for women marrying for the first time was 25.9.

The median age at first marriage for men has changed, too:

In 1900, it was 25.9.
In 1950, it fell to 22.8.
In 1998, it rose to 26.7.
In 2006, the median age for men marrying for the first time was 27.5.

because he didn't talk enough. I thought he was totally turned off by my babble. I was surprised when he IM'ed me the next night. We had a few more dates in restaurants, and then he invited me to his place for dinner.

On the evening of the big date at his place, one of the biggest blizzards in years was gearing up to hit Boston. I tried to cancel, but he refused. He told me to take the train up to his place, or he'd pick me up. I got a cab (the driver told me I was his last fare of the evening—driving was too bad) and then took the train to Pat's place, about fifteen miles outside the city. He picked me up and brought me back to his place, where he'd begun to prepare chicken parmesan. We ate dinner, kissed, watched television, and talked until one in the morning, at which time . . . I asked him to drive me home.

Yep. I asked him to drive me home. Worst blizzard in approximately twenty-five years, and I asked him to drive me home. Three bedrooms at his place, and I asked him to drive me home. Know what? He did it, without hesitation or question. And he still called me the next day. That was the beginning of something for me.

I had a really hard time with the relationship when things first got started. My last relationship had ended with a broken engagement, and I was terrified of getting hurt again; I really put him through the wringer. But he was so understanding, probably because he had been through something very similar. He had been married briefly, and his marriage ended very badly. He was so hurt, and I think we were just about at the same place when we met. We were very cautious, but we knew something was there worth exploring.

I never thought I'd be happy. I knew that marriage to my ex would have been miserable because he was a miserable person. But I accepted the misery—I thought that's what relationships were. I can't imagine my life without Patrick. I know how lucky I am that we found each other, and he tells me how lucky he is every day.

advice for others
give everyone a chance.

We had both been though a lot—my broken engagement, his divorce. We were both very cautious, but we approached things very differently. He kept telling himself, "She's not my ex-wife, and I can't assume she'll act the same way." I kept telling myself, "He has to prove that he's not my ex-fiancé." My advice? Give everyone a chance. I was unsure about Pat a few dates in, and I'm positive that he thought I was completely nuts many, many times. Keep your own life going—don't allow yourself to get completely sucked in. I had a history of losing myself in my relationships, and when they ended, I'd wind up completely alone, save a few very good friends who always stuck by me. No one is perfect, and everyone has a past. Don't be ashamed of your own past, and don't judge someone else's.

quote/ unquote	"I think men who have a pierced ear are better prepared for marriage. They've experienced pain and bought jewelry."
	—Rita Rudner

how kevin *met* julie

Met Online: January 2006

Met in Person: Valentine's Day 2006, in St. Cloud, Florida. Kevin was twenty-four and Julie was twenty-six.

Married: June 2007

Until I was five years old, I was so thin you could see my ribs through my skin. I kept getting tonsillitis, but after I got my tonsils out, it didn't hurt to eat anymore. So I kept eating and eating and getting chubbier and chubbier. I lost some weight in college, but when I graduated, I didn't make the wisest choices when it came to food. I would have frozen dinners for lunch and on the way home I would stop at McDonalds! On January 1, 2006, I told myself, "Heart attacks run in the family. I can't keep doing this to myself. I am going to lose weight."

I joined Weight Watchers on January 13. After my first Weight Watchers meeting, I went home and joined an online weight loss message board. That's how I met Julie. She sent me an instant message and said, "Hey, what's up," and noticed we both had the same starting weight, 307 pounds. She sent me before and after pictures. First of all, she was beautiful and second, the transition was amazing.

When I met Julie, I had been in a relationship with someone for four years. However, things had been deteriorating really quickly in recent months. We were arguing all the time, and she didn't support me when I decided to start losing weight. I would focus on making healthy meals, and she would eat fast food in front of me.

I didn't want to cheat on my girlfriend, and so I didn't want to get too flirtatious with Julie, but I liked her. We e-mailed each other to offer support during our weight loss. After a couple weeks, when we started talking on the phone, we shared more personal stories. She told me she was waiting for someone who was worth her time, and I liked that.

The first time I really remember doing anything flirtatious we were on the phone and I said, "I don't know if this is okay or not, but I have a pretty good feeling that I love you." This was three weeks in and I hadn't even met her. I just had the feeling. We just had a certain connection, so I don't think she was surprised. She told me she loved me, too.

I lived in Des Moines, Iowa, and she lived in St. Cloud, Florida. The day before Valentine's Day, I called and asked if it would be all right if I came to visit her. She said, "Okay, when are you thinking of coming?" I said, "Valentine's Day." And she said, "Tomorrow?" After I bought the ticket, I broke up with my girlfriend.

Meeting for the first time was a bit awkward. Julie was inviting a stranger into her house, and I was flying from Iowa to Florida to meet a stranger. When the plane landed in Orlando, I called her and said, "Where are you?" She said, "I'm coming up the escalator." I immediately recognized her from the pic-

marriage in biblical times

According to Deuteronomy 24:5, a married man is exempt from the army for a full year so he can stay home and "gladden" his wife.

tures she sent me. I ran to her with my arms stretched out. We hugged and kissed. When I got off that plane, it was love at first sight. I always said it couldn't happen, but I saw her and I knew it could.

advice for others
marry someone you can talk to.

I have never gotten along with anyone as well as I do with Julie. In other relationships, even with my guy friends, I get so mad sometimes. If I get mad at her for some stupid reason, I look at her and just think, "I can't get mad at you!" I know we are going to last forever. In the state of Florida, a couple is required to go through marriage counseling before getting married. You take a test, and they tell you things you should be able to talk about. The other night we talked about religion and having kids for two and a half hours. I thought, "If we can sit here and talk and work things out like this, we can work anything out."

we were only kids

*A*re you one of those people who rises in the morning with clothes already laid out for the day, a sandwich with lettuce peeking out the edges ready and bagged in the fridge, and the gym bag packed by the door? Because I'm not. And I suspect that it may be these people, the ones whose hair drapes the way it did the day it was cut in the salon and who never end up with coffee on their shirts as they race for the bus, who had the presence of mind—the prescience, even—to see ahead to the days when skipping would be passé and life would be about more than trading stickers. I have a theory that these boys and girls were calm enough children to look up from their coloring and think, "That girl cradling the dolly would make a lovely mother." Or "That boy has an excellent way with his safety scissors, and I think I feel for him in a way I may not yet understand but feels pretty cool."

The rest of us were finger painting up a storm in crinkly plastic smocks or determinedly hammering square pegs into round holes while around us little hands were linking. Not all those who met as kids knew right away, of course. But that makes it even sweeter. Because whenever the romance begins, the strong foundation is already there. He knows my parents, she knows I like blue snow cones. And a home, a life, is built from there.

how susie *met* andrew

Met: 1969 in Greensboro, North Carolina

Married: February 2002

Our dads were roommates in the sixties at the University of North Carolina dental school. They may have even known each other before—they both grew up in small towns in North Carolina. Andrew and I have really known each other since birth. Greensboro is small; everybody knows everybody. Our parents were at each other's weddings. My mom had never been to New York until his parents married. She says it was the fanciest wedding she had ever seen. Andrew's parents have a picture of me as a newborn, still in the hospital, and on the back of it my father had written, "Susan, seven hours old. Hope Andrew will come to meet her soon." His parents even came to my first wedding.

Andrew is a year older than I am. We were at each other's birthday parties, went to the same Jewish day school, performed in the Chanukah play together. We were in the same high school, but we ran in very different crowds. I belonged to BBYO (a national Jewish youth organization), and he was on the football team. We'd say hello to each other in the hall, but we were weren't socially friendly.

The years went by. I ended up moving to Atlanta. Andrew had gone to Emory in Atlanta and had stayed on after graduation. I was looking at apartments and condos in the neighborhood where my parents knew that Andrew happened to own a townhouse. They said, "Call Andrew and talk about the neighborhood."

I called Andrew just to chat: "I'm moving here, what do you think of this neighborhood?" He had been seeing a girlfriend, not Jewish but very serious, for a number of years. Within the first month after I moved here, I went out to dinner with a friend and we met up with the two of them for dessert.

Time went by, I don't know how much, and I heard that Andrew had broken up with his girlfriend. I saw his parents at the gym when I was back home in North Carolina for a visit. "He's fine," they told me. "Just a little lonely." Even then, I had no thoughts of him in a romantic sense.

I had been in Atlanta a year when I joined JDate, a Jewish online dating site. Unexpectedly, I got an e-mail from Andrew. All it said was, "Hey Susie, saw you on JDate. Just joined. How does this thing work?"

I didn't know if he was hitting on me or being funny. I was totally panicked: Andrew is trying to ask me out! I carefully decided what to write—I even discussed it with my mother. "Hey Andrew, JDate is funny, let's meet for lunch. I have a lot

| **quote/** **unquote** | "[I knew she was the one] the moment I saw her. When she walked past my history class, I was immediately smitten . . . When I first saw Cori, I wanted to meet the cheerleader. It wasn't until I graduated from college that I knew I wanted to be with her forever." |
| | —Brad Meltzer on meeting his wife, as quoted on his website (*www.bradmeltzer.com*) |

of cute girlfriends I can set you up with." We met for burritos on a Tuesday night—very casual.

We ended up hanging out a lot. We volunteered together, saw each other at the Jewish film festival. He liked to hike, so we went hiking. It was still very platonic. He would tell me about girls he was dating, and I would tell him about dates I had.

One night we went to see the movie *Bridget Jones's Diary*. He picked me up, we went to the movies, and he brought me home. He walked me in—a very polite Southern boy. We were standing in my living room and he said, "Can I ask you something? We always have such a good time together. Would it be okay if I asked you out on a real date?" I said, "Sure." We decided to go to the zoo. In the meantime, my uncle had given me to tickets to see Billy Joel, so I asked if he wanted to go. It was in a couple of days, before the zoo date, so the Billy Joel concert was our first date.

By April 2001 we were officially a couple, but I didn't tell my parents, and he didn't tell his. I didn't even tell some of my friends. I had a feeling it could be something but I didn't want to talk about it.

A few months later, in June, my brother and future sister-in-law came home to North Carolina for a visit. My brother's wedding was in September, and that weekend in June my parents hounded me. "Are you inviting Andrew to the wedding?" I said, "I don't know!" It seemed like such a bold move. I did ask him the following week. My mom reserved two hotel rooms for us and I finally told her, "You can cancel one of the rooms."

advice for others
it's about friendship.

Underneath it all, what matters most is that someone can be your friend. People are often initially attracted to the way someone looks or maybe how much money they have. But deep down, what you need is someone you can have fun with. Andrew's my best friend. After the honeymoon is over and you're trying to create a life together, you need someone you feel most comfortable with.

how bev *met* gordie

Met: 1955 in Glen Flora, Wisconsin.

Married: November 1974

We were born in 1955, and have pretty much known each other ever since then. Our families were in the same church, and from the time we were little kids our older brothers and sisters kind of pushed us together. This was in Glen Flora, Wisconsin, population ninety-six. It's where we were born and raised. We've put down roots so deep, I don't think we'll ever leave here.

Gordie actually proposed to me in writing in the first grade. I still remember the note; I wish I had kept the dumb thing. I didn't give him an answer until the end of the day, and he later said he was nervous all day and his stomach hurt. Neither of us can remember if he asked again or if I volunteered my answer. It was all by paper; I slid back the note saying "Yes."

We kind of dated from eighth grade on. Our parents wouldn't let us really date that early, but we hung around together at the 4-H club and at church events. I took piano lessons from his aunt. While I waited for my sister to finish her lesson, we'd sit together on a bale of hay. When our parents would let us, our older brothers and sisters took us with them when they went on dates. We officially started dating at sixteen.

Even though we were young, we were already planning our future together. After both attending tech school, Gordie got into the family business. We married one year later and signed a buy/sell agreement on his family business the next year.

Now, as adults, we own a business. We share an office, go on business trips together, and have worked sided by side our entire lives, twenty-four/seven. One of the reasons we have gotten along so well is that even though we married young, we really had a long courtship. Finding a mate can be a complicated thing—we were really lucky.

advice for others
know and like each other.

Be sure you really know that person well. You cannot go into it thinking you are going to change the other person. Be sure it's not the honeymoon period, and follow your gut. Little things that grate on you while you date are going to kill you when you're married.

how priscilla *met* scott

Met: August 1995 in Clinton, Missouri

Married: August 2003

We lived in the same small town of about 10,000 people. We had the same kindergarten teacher, but I went in the morning while Scott went in the afternoon. Our town had just one elementary school, one middle school, one high school; we were in school our whole lives together.

We had different teachers until the fifth grade. Our friendship started in sixth grade. I don't know what attracted me to him other than that he was really nice. I don't think our parents had ever met. His parents owned a small business, and my dad did too. So they knew of each other through business, but not by name.

When we got to the eighth grade we started talking more, but we really weren't dating. We would do stuff with our friends, typical middle school stuff. He went to a small church on the edge of town and he came to the youth group activities on Wednesday nights at my church.

While in high school, we had a homecoming dance and we were thinking, "We both need a date and we're good friends, so why don't we go together?" I remember we had that conversation the third day of our freshman year in August 1999. He called me that night and his exact words were, "What if I want to go as more than friends?" And I said, "Well, that would be more than okay." We both realized we had mutual feelings.

We decided to go on a date and not wait for the dance; homecoming was in October, and he wanted to take me out for my birthday in September. We went out with another couple for pizza and bowling. We couldn't drive yet, so we had our parents drop us off and pick us up at the pizza place. Kind of lame, but we were only fifteen.

I remember slow dancing with him at the homecoming dance. It was in the cafeteria where there was a stage area where they could put the DJ and we could dance on the floor. It was kind of nerve-wracking because we had been friends for so long, but now our relationship was changing. I remember our first kiss vividly. We were at the movies with another couple. We had dated for a while but we still hadn't kissed. We were young and probably both scared, to be honest.

what's in the water?

Mathematically speaking, those who marry young have a better chance of celebrating their silver and gold anniversaries than those who meet later in life. But can they match these powerhouses? As reported on Wikipedia.com, these couples have each been married more than eighty-one years:

John Rocchip and Amelia Antonelli
of Rhode Island married February 10, 1923.

Orbin Jack Hoffer and Dorothy Stahly
of Indiana married February 14, 1921.

Martin and Christina Terry
of South Carolina married February 7, 1924.

Gilbert Hill and Sadie E. Longmoor
of Florida married June 15, 1920.

As I got older and started learning about dating, I knew I didn't want to date someone I wouldn't consider marrying. Then I thought about whether I would consider marrying Scott and I thought, "Yeah, I would."

When we were sixteen, Scott came down with strep throat and I brought him a stuffed gorilla with "I love you" written on it. I was sitting on the edge of his bed. He gave me a little gift book of love quotes. I don't remember what led up to it, but he said, "I was thinking a lot today and I was wondering what you thought about getting married." I was shocked and I said, "When were you thinking?" and he said, "Right after high school."

When I realized we shared the same feelings about marriage, I was unbelievably happy, but it wasn't just some fairy-tale story to us. All through high school we were maturing and seeing other people going in and out of relationships, but we were together the whole time. We were definitely the odd ones out.

In December of our senior year, we went to his house and for the first time he showed me a tree in the back yard where he had carved our initials really early into our dating. It was cold out, and he was wearing his letterman jacket. He had his hands in his pockets. Then he pulled out the ring and proposed and of course I said yes.

We went together and told his family and then went to my house and told my parents. My parents were fine with it. I know some people would say we were too young, but my mom and dad were nineteen when they married, and my older sister was nineteen when she got married, too. I was surprised and a little nervous that he proposed so early, but I was very happy.

That summer his parents separated. Their divorce made it really hard on us and made us really think about our decision. He thought, "If they can't make it work, how am I going to make it work at eighteen?" His parents owned a business together and they fought over it constantly. From their fighting, Scott learned that we needed to work together to make our marriage strong. We had already planned to move to Kentucky for college, which would get us out of the middle of the divorce. We had people telling us that we should wait, and a lot of people warned us that "You never know a person before you live together," but we didn't.

We got married on a Saturday, took a short honeymoon, then got back to town and got our stuff together and moved to Kentucky the next Saturday to go to college.

advice for others

marriage is about maturity and complementing each other.

I would go back to the line of "Don't date anyone you wouldn't consider marrying." It's just a waste of your time. You don't want to give a piece of yourself emotionally to someone you can't commit to. Age doesn't really matter as much as maturity does. You can be twenty-five and be immature and not be able to make a marriage work. And you can be nineteen and understand how to work through your differences.

---

how **sue**
met **ron**

Met: 1952 in Queens, New York. Sue was ten and Ron was twelve.
Married: September 1962

On September 9, 2007, my husband and I celebrated our forty-fifth wedding anniversary. We met in 1952 when his family moved into apartment 4F in Mitchell Gardens, Flushing, Queens. My family had recently moved into apartment 4E in the same building.

I was an only child; Ron had an older brother. I had a lot of cousins but no siblings, which is what I really wanted. I wanted someone to confide in. I was hoping girls would move in. When Ron's family did instead, I thought, "Well, okay. Better than nothing."

Ron was a nerd, a bookworm. I was a chubby kid who was also more scholarly than athletic. He was much more interested in science and making bombs—I certainly was not into that at all. We shared a wall in common, our living room wall. His mother got annoyed at me for knocking on his front door all the time, so I decided we should have a signal. I put a pencil sharpener in the closet. If I wanted him to come over, I would sharpen a pencil. My mother would come into the closet and say, "What are you doing?"

It was very platonic. I used to joke years later that I had to marry him because he did my Latin homework. Whatever courses he took, I would take, and because I never did as well as he did, he did my homework. He would tell me about his girlfriends and I'd tell him about boys I liked, those who liked me, those who didn't. We confided our feelings to each other.

But when he asked another girl to his senior prom, I was crushed, absolutely crushed. I think that was the beginning of my true feelings for him. He thought he was infatuated with her and then she dumped him. He came back to me and we cried together and that brought us closer. I tease him that someday he has to take me to a prom.

Ron went to Queens College and I went ahead and graduated high school a semester early because I didn't want to be

marriage
in biblical
times

If a man has sexual relations with a virgin, he must marry her and he can't ever divorce her. (Deuteronomy 22:29)

another way to go about it

"The female mite known as *Histionstoma muchiei* creates her own husband from scratch. She lays eggs that turn into male adults without needing to be fertilized. The mother then copulates with her own sons within three or four days of laying the eggs, after which the sons die rather quickly."
—David Wallechinsky and Amy Wallace, *The New Book of Lists: The Original Compendium of Curious Information*

without him. After college, he won scholarships to graduate school. The most prestigious was to the University of Washington in Seattle. Neither of us had the financial wherewithal to go back and forth. I was in my sophomore year at Queens, and the thought of our being so far apart for several years was unbearable. So we decided to get married. I was nineteen and Ron was twenty-one. We thought we'd go to Washington together.

Everyone thought we were crazy and that the marriage wouldn't last. I was the first grandchild to get married. His mother was quite verbal about my being an only child and how I must be spoiled and demanding and he won't finish school. She was wrong because my husband now has multiple PhDs. Before she passed away, his mother apologized to me. She said that I wasn't demanding and that I was in fact quite supportive of his studies, as he was of mine.

Before we even moved to Washington, he won a full scholarship to Princeton so we ended up staying on the East Coast, but we kept our plans to get married. My mother, a liberal thinker, said, "If you want to cancel the wedding you can go out to New Jersey on the weekends and sleep with him. You're only nineteen." I said, "Mom, I'm not that kind of girl." There were two types when I was young.

For years I was a little jealous of the woman he took to the prom. About eleven years ago, she contacted Ron and said she and her husband would like to meet with us so she could explain why she dumped Ron. It had always been on her mind. I had a meeting that night. I said, "I can't go, but why don't you? I'll meet you for dessert." So we did. When we came home he said, "I'm really glad I chose you." And I said, "Me, too." We've known each other fifty-five years and we are still best friends.

advice for others
be lighthearted.

One thing we learned, and we learned it from each other, is that you can't take life seriously. Even in the darkest hours, you have to say, "I'm going to learn something from this and something better is going to happen." You have to be optimistic about your life and your marriage. Death is inevitable. You want to have as much joy in your life as possible. That doesn't mean you are going to be happy all the time. There are spurts and stops, and when there are stops, you have to know there is a horizon.

When people would ask us how long we've been married, we used to joke, "About twenty-five good years." Which is true. And we've been married forty-five years! Do I love him all the time? No. Sometimes I really hate his guts. But sometimes I look at him and it's a Sunday morning and he's making coffee and we're going to do the crossword puzzle and I think he's the most wonderful person in the world. And sometimes I wake up and look over and say, "What am I doing here?"

we were
meant to be

*M*any of us can remember some variation of the puppet show in which one puppet is looking for another puppet, and the second puppet is close by, but the first puppet doesn't notice him. The first puppet says something like, "I thought he was here a minute ago," and the kids in the audience rise up on their knees in squealing panic, yelling, "He's there!" and "Behind you!" or "Look!" all the while jabbing the air with their stubby little fingers in an effort to point the way for the clueless puppet.

And the puppet—I remember him with a dopey voice and a purple velvet sleeve for a body—turns his face toward the audience and says, "Huh? What did you say? Right here?" while the kids are in apoplexies of helpfulness and the other puppet—maybe he's a squirrel bandit with a sack over his shoulder—sneaks over to the far side of the puppet stage.

Romance can be like that. You both go to the same high school, but your crowds sit on opposite sides of the cafeteria. You go to some of the same parties in your early twenties, but, inevitably, he's making out with some squirrel bandit and you're knocking back drinks. (Or something like that.) You can—like my sister Deborah and her husband John—have me in common, but just not know it.

But when it's meant to be, these couples find, it's meant to be. Even when it takes many years of missed connections before you both turn around at the same time and see each other standing there, as you had been all along.

how **rose** *met* **mike**

Met: June 1999 in Providence, Rhode Island. Rose was thirty-five and Mike was thirty-seven.

Married: September 2002

I had been divorced for maybe six or seven years when I started going to the gym. I was lifting weights when I met the man who would become my husband. During a break in my sets, he came up to me and said, "Can I step in while you're resting?" I said, "Absolutely," and jokingly he said, "Oooh, I don't know if I can handle the weight you've got on here." So right away I could tell he was a big funny wise guy.

We ran into each other a lot at the gym and would always talk. Sometimes he'd help me with the sets and I knew right away that I liked this guy. I really liked him, but I sort of intuitively knew it wasn't the right time, that neither one of us was ready to do anything about that, so we just kind of left it the way it was.

I had recently decided to change careers. I had been working at a credit union for thirteen years and I decided to quit my job and go to school for aesthetics. That meant I had to quit going to the gym because I was putting myself through school and had to cut back on expenses. But I thought about Mike all the time. I used to say, "You know, Mikey might have been have been the one that got away." When I drove by the gym, I always wondered if he was in there.

It took me about ten months to complete school and during that time my brothers and I started doing yoga in Mystic, Connecticut, about twenty minutes from the gym where I had met Mikey. I did yoga on and off for a few months, and then one Friday he showed up in my class. There were maybe fifty people there. I looked across the room. We saw each other and I just looked at him, and I knew. That was it, I just knew. We picked up right where we left off and he started teasing me right away.

He asked me to take tennis lessons with him and I said, "You know what? I can't do it, it won't fit into my schedule." Then he asked me to take swing dance lessons with him—and then I really knew he was the one. We started dating. We'd do our swing dance class and we'd come back to my place, he'd

quote/ unquote

"I married him in 1964. Of course this marriage took place before we became acquainted with each other, since as was the practice of religious families of those days, his mother came to our house to propose and after the usual discussions the marriage ceremonies were performed."
—Mrs. Khamenei, wife of Ayatollah Khamenei, Supreme Leader of Iran, as quoted in *The Magazine for Muslim Women*, 1992

buy dinner and clean up or I'd cook for us and he'd clean up, and that was it—we knew.

I was young the first time I married. I met my ex-husband at twenty-one and I was twenty-five when we got married. I think part of the reason I went with that particular guy was that he was something familiar. He was Italian, just like me. He had the same background. It was kind of easy. I thought I loved him but now realize it wasn't love.

I think I married him basically to get out of the house. All my friends were getting married; people around me were starting families. For me, I didn't really want to start a family right away, but it was the next step. It was what I was supposed to do. I never felt it was the right thing for me though and it ended my marriage.

But Mike is the other half of me, there is just no doubt about it. I'll be thinking of a song and he'll hum it or actually start singing the song. It happens all the time. He knows when

when knocking heads is a good thing

In Galicnik, Macedonia, "[o]n St. Peter's Day each year a multiple wedding feast is held...The most interesting feature of the wedding ceremony itself is that brides, bridegrooms, and guest knock their heads together. The first night of the marriage is spent in a complicated hide-and-seek game and the newlyweds do not sleep together. There is a great feast on the second day and that night the marriages are consummated."

—*Holidays, Festivals, and Celebrations of the World Dictionary, Third Edition*

I'm cold without my even saying it—if I get in bed, he tucks the sheet in just right where I was cold. It sounds stupid but he really does complete me. And every time I talk about it, I cry. I feel so lucky to have found him.

He just takes care of me like nobody ever has. I have always been the caretaker. It's so nice to know I don't have to work that hard. This relationship is easy and we truly are friends. I can't describe it any other way. He was so kind, gentle, and sweet that I didn't believe he was true at first. But I took a chance on the good boy, not the bad boy (for a change) and it was the best choice I ever made. He is my best friend. It's the way it should be and I never in my life thought that I would have that. I'm lucky. I know that and I'm very grateful.

advice for others

know yourself—and be sure your partner knows you, too.

With Mike I could always be myself. I never had to hide any part of myself from him. Not hiding any bit of who you are to that other person, even the not-so-nice parts, to me that was huge. He always used to say to me, "Are you being yourself?"

I met Mike at a time in my life when I was taking care of myself. Knowing who you are and what you want out of life is important. I met someone who didn't need any caretaking; he just wanted to love me. We made sure that both of our needs were met and still are.

Knowing that you deserve a good person in your life is key to a healthy relationship. When you can be in a heated argument one minute and laughing the next, when you come home from work and your feet hurt and someone just starts rubbing them without asking, when someone finishes your thoughts, when someone starts singing a song you were just thinking of, when you can't wait to come home to see that man's smile and have him wrap his arms around you, kiss you and say, "I missed you today." I never thought I would find a love like that but if I did so can a lot of other people. Just keep your faith in the Divine, and never close your eyes to all the miracles that happen to us every day.

how dixie *met* bobby

Met: October 1995 in Natchitoches, Louisiana. Dixie was fifty-nine and Bobby was fifty-six.

Married: August 1996

In the 1950s, we both lived in Austin, Texas. Even though we lived in the same city, we didn't know each other. Later we both lived many miles away in Midland. Again, we didn't know each other. In the 1990s, I was living in Natchitoches, Louisiana, and he was working on an oil rig there and once again we never met. He and his wife lived two doors down from my mother in a gated community. I had never heard my mother speak of them.

I moved back in with my mother in Natchitoches to take care of her, and while I was there, Bobby's wife passed away.

wedding anniversary gifts

How well do you know the anniversary gifts—traditional and modern? Take this quiz to find out.

1. Name any two of the traditional anniversary gifts for the first five years of marriage.

2. Which of the following is not a modern equivalent for an anniversary gift?
   a. Appliances
   b. Fur
   c. Original poetry
   d. Real estate
   e. Commissioned nude portrait of oneself
   f. Books

3. In the traditional system, in which years is a gift not given?
   a. 16
   b. 17
   c. 18
   d. 19

4. True or false: The gold anniversary celebrates twenty-five years of marriage.

5. In the modern system, which precious gem can be given in as many as eight anniversary years?

Three weeks after she died, I went to the office to get a new gate opener and that's when I finally met Bobby after all these years. We had a long conversation until finally I told him I had to get to work. I didn't give many details but I said, "I have a shop."

Somehow he found me, and we spent a whole afternoon getting to know each other. When a customer came in, he'd just look around and then we'd start talking again.

I had been single for thirteen years. I was married at seventeen—way too young—and stayed married for over twenty years. He had been happily married for thirty-six years when his wife died. Besides taking care of my mother, I was running a good business. A man was the last thing on my mind. But I found Bobby so interesting, and he liked me a whole lot.

The second time he saw me he told me he was going to marry me at some point. I said, "I don't think so." But within a few weeks, I was thinking, "This man is special." We did not have sex before we married. It's unusual in today's time to wait, but Bobby felt that we would have a closer relationship if we didn't. And I think he was right. It was just a decision Bobby and I made between ourselves.

To be honest, we didn't go out that much. He would come over and spend time with my ninety-four year old mother and me, just talking. The first time we actually went out on a date, it was a whole lot of fun. They had just opened a Barnes & Noble in Tyler, Texas, and I had never been to one. I told Bobby there was a new bookstore opening not too far away and said I would like to go. He said, "Sure." We went straight to the comedy section and read Jeff Foxworthy's book *You*

marriage in biblical times

Back in the olden days, the groom's family had to pay a bride-price to the bride's father. Possibly the oddest bride-price on record can be found in Genesis 34. Shechem wanted to marry Dinah—after he had already slept with her. Before they would allow it, Dinah's family required that he and all his fellow townsmen be circumcised.

Alas, it was only a ruse. When the men were recovering, Dinah's brothers came to the town and killed every last man.

Might Be A Redneck If. It's a wonder they didn't throw us out, we were laughing so loudly.

We read to each other until two in the morning, first in the store and then back at his place. It is one of my favorite memories of us. I don't think we've laughed that much since. We had just discovered each other, too, and you know how you are—we were a little giddy. We had only known each other a month when we went out on that first date. I liked him, but I was just happy with my single life—I was perfectly happy the way I was.

Bobby loves to ride his motorcycle; he learned when he was about ten years old. He had a motorcycle, of course, when we married. After we'd been married a couple of years, he asked if I would ride one, and I said, "I don't think so." He talked me into sitting on one and I was petrified. We were married in 1996—in 1999 I started riding. We took three trips on a two-wheel and I finally told him, "Bobby, I'm going to be honest with you. I am a wreck." And I've never been scared of anything in my life. I was always the one who said, "Let's do it, it'll be fun."

He had the bike converted it into a trike. Ten thousand dollars he just dished out so I would ride. And then it sat in the garage for a year. One day he gave me an ultimatum. He was just sitting at the table and said, "I'm going to tell you something. In Madison, Wisconsin, they are having their Wingding"—I thought it was a cupcake. It's a huge rally that the Gold Wing Road Riders Association has every year—"and you can go or you can stay at home, but I'm going."

My stomach dropped. Everything I do, I pray. I prayed about it. And the Lord was telling me, "It's going to be okay." I fell in love with riding and I have loved it ever since. We have been all over the country on a motorcycle. We have ridden Route 83 from Brownsville, Texas, all the way to Canada. We rode from Texas all through Alaska. We've ridden through all fifty states.

During our long rides, I thought a lot. I would wish there was something we could do for others, and this is the honest-to-goodness truth: I was lying in bed one night sound asleep and all of a sudden I just raised up in the bed and it was like the spirit of God was all over me. God told me, "Your husband loves riding a motorcycle and if you will ride a motorcycle with him and feed the needy, I will protect you." I sometimes hesitate to tell people about that, but we have never once come close to having something happen to us. It was God speaking to me.

Now we deliver food to the needy. I composed a letter to other members of the Gold Wing Road Riders Association and told them we had this charity, Fun Riders. I said we would be coming through their town and asked if they would meet us to accept some food for their church or charity. We've ridden through all fifty states, leaving food for charity on church steps.

advice for others

don't smother each other.

We like to travel, and of course we have the motorcycles. But we also let each other do our own thing. He plays golf three times a week and that is great with me. I garden and go to Bible study. We let each other have our own space.

how jen *met* matt

Met: January 1998 in Orangeburg, New York. Both Jen and Matt were twenty-three.

Married: December 2001

My brother Jamie and his wife went to college with Matt's brother and sister-in-law. I knew the four of them well, but Matt and I didn't know each other. Five years after college, the four of them started hanging out together again and got a shore house. I would go visit and Matt would go visit, but we never were there at the same time. Everyone told me, "You two should get together," but it never seemed to happen. Eventually, Matt's sister-in-law said to me, "You two are like ships that pass in the night." She told Matt we should get together and he said something along the lines of, "Whatever, okay, sure."

We were together at a lot of places at the same time but never knew it. I had gone to college with a lot of people he went to high school with. We grew up in the same county. I know a specific Christmas party where we both were, but we didn't see each other, the month before I actually met him. We went to the same bar all the time. It was a bar where everyone went when they were home from college. Finally, Matt's brother and sister-in-law had a Super Bowl party and told him, "Listen, we're going to bring Jen over. It will be casual."

When I finally met Matt, there was an instant connection. It was completely different from meeting other guys. I was so comfortable. We sat in a corner and talked the whole time. Honest to God, I don't remember what we talked about. We just sat down together. Everyone else sat down to eat dinner, but we stayed where we were. I don't even remember who won the Super Bowl.

Like a typical guy, it took him a while to call me. He also wasn't very consistent with the phone calls. One week he'd call, and then two weeks would go by before he called again. He'd call on a Saturday to go out on a Saturday night. It was annoying, but I hung in there despite what my friends told me I should do, which was blow him off. When we did go out, we would go to a bar and stand in the corner and just talk, just the two of us. People used to make fun of us.

Things got more serious when we decided to go to Aruba for vacation together. While we were there, he said something

that made me think. He said to me, "If I was going to propose, this is the setting it would happen in." He was one of
those people who never wanted to really talk about getting
married. Not that I wanted to; I wasn't rushing to get married.
I didn't think we had been together long enough. I felt that
I was still too young, and I didn't think I was ready. I knew we
loved each other but hadn't thought about how things would
go over the long term.

I remember going to the bathroom and looking in the mirror and thinking, "Oh gosh, this is something here." I felt he
was one of the good ones, and he proved me right. A lot of
that feeling came from knowing his family. I wasn't meeting a
stranger. We almost had the interview process finished before
we even met.

I don't necessarily believe we were meant to meet each
other. I don't think there is one person in the world for you.
But compared to other relationships, I think I met the right
one. I think we each actually found the right person.

advice for others
matchmaking is good.

If someone thinks they have someone for you, you should get
out there, even when you think it might not work. I did, and
I realized the worst thing that could happen is that nothing
happens. Meeting through family has helped us through what
might have been difficulties—and family gatherings are really
nice.

how deborah *met* john

Met: November 2000 in New York City, New York. Deborah was twenty-seven and John was thirty-one.

Married: March 2002

Our moms both read the same article on speed dating in *The New York Times,* and both said we should go. So we both went to an event at the Hard Rock Café in Manhattan. With speed dating, a bunch of people get together, male and female. You meet everybody in the group, but you only have seven minutes to talk to each person. One guy I talked to was really weird. He asked where I was from and then talked about the number of letters in the name of the town. And I thought, "You are really wacko."

Later in the evening, I met John. He seemed like such a nice person from the minute he sat down. I asked him what he did and he said he was an internist and a pediatrician. I said, "Oh, you're a pediatrician. No wonder you have such a nice smile." I asked him where he worked, and he told me the name of the hospital. I said, "I know someone there, a friend of my sister's. Do you know her?" And he said, "I don't know her well, but I went to high school with her college roommate." And I said, "Where?" And he told me and I said, "That's my sister! You know her!"

I think we spent the rest of the time talking about my sister (Rachel Safier, the author of this book). I thought John was extremely nice and refreshing, but I didn't know if I liked him. Still, I put him down on the list of people I'd agree to a date with.

During the break, John was standing with another girl. He called over to me, "I hope I see you again." This girl he was standing with looked extremely possessive so I thought maybe he would call, maybe he wouldn't. As soon as I came home I called my sister, and I told her I met John there. She said he was nice and nerdy. I said, "Good!" I liked that he wasn't one of the rebellious kids at her school.

John asked me for a real date three days after our speed-dating encounter. He told me he was going to find me hell

under your spell

According to *Sister Moon's Spell Castings: Practical Magick for Daily Life*, which of the following is needed to "bring a new romantic love into your life?"

A. Eye of newt, a cauldron (or a kettle), four drops of morning dew, and several grains of sand.
B. Something blue (the darker the better), a written wish, a hair from an old wise man, and a cup of orange (or lemon) zest.
C. Three pink candles, Algiers oil, Pink Musk incense, thirteen strips of pink material that are at least seven inches long and two inches wide, and a permanent marker.
D. One robin's egg, two blades of grass, three fall leaves, and a thimble of sea water.

Answer: D. And remember, Sister Moon warns, "whenever casting love spells, remember to make sure that your intentions are not obsessive. Extend energy only to persons who are worthy of your love."

or high water; he had been planning to look my sister up and call her if I hadn't picked him. After talking for a while, we realized we had even more in common. We went to the same elementary school. We were at so many of the same events, like Rachel's performance of *Oklahoma* in fifth grade and her high school graduation. I always thought Rachel's friends were

love in the kitchen

As award-winning executive chef of the popular New York City restaurant Butter, Alexandra Guarnaschelli regularly hosts such celebrities as Madonna, Demi Moore and Ashton Kutcher, and Penelope Cruz. Guarnaschelli met her husband when he took her class on preparing fish, and I asked for her thoughts on cooking and love. Here's what she said.

"I would liken relationships to sauce making and not to baking. In baking, you mix all the ingredients together and put it into the oven, and once it's in the oven you can't fix it. You can't take out a quarter tablespoon of something, you can't take out the lemon zest. Even sometimes right when the pan hits the rack and you slide it gently into the oven you already want to change something, but you can't. It's irreparable. Then you have to sit by the oven and see what's wrong. With sauce, you can pretty much change anything. Playing with different ingredients offers you lots of freedom. It's like a relationship. Sometimes you think, 'Wow, I can't get a handle, I can't make it go deeper.' Or, 'Wow, I have all these different tools at my disposal at different times and can potentially change what I'm doing.' You can be more open to accepting limitations or experimenting so next time you make it better. You can reinvent yourself and make a better partner out of yourself—and a better sauce."

nice; they really cared about her. I wanted friends like hers, and I thought, "Oh, this is one of the good guys."

He was the first person I was ever with who made me feel completely comfortable. I liked being with him. I thought he was smart and funny and handsome. He was just very easy to be with. When my dad met him later, he loved him (and he wasn't that easy to impress). Even my brother, who doesn't like anybody, liked him. After our first date, I actually thought, "This isn't somebody to take lightly. This is a serious person." I tease him that he was easy to marry.

But sometimes I'd get scared. John was my first serious boyfriend, and I wasn't used to all the attention I was getting from him. He called me once when I was visiting my parents even though I hadn't given him the number. It freaked me out, and I told him to leave me alone. I used to pack my bags to go over to his place and then later in the evening I'd just pick up and go home.

But at the same time, I was tired of going out with guys who weren't important to me, and John was so nice. He was very reliable—I knew I could always count on him. He was a decent person, wasn't jerking me around. Being scared was just me being dumb. I'm very used to my own space. I like my time alone sometimes. I calmed down after about three months. John told me he loved me sometime that spring. But he wouldn't talk marriage yet. I'd sing, "John, I'm glad you're here, I hope that you don't disappear. Your grandma thinks I'm okay. When's it going to be my wedding day?" And he'd answer, "Not yet."

As we got closer to thinking about getting married, it mattered to me that he had regular work hours, especially if we were going to have kids. In fact, he was the first person I ever met whom I could envision as father of my children. I remember saying to one of my friends that he would be a wonderful father. (Our son is now three, and John *is* a wonderful dad. He's patient and energetic, and I'm not the only one getting up at all hours.) And John seemed like an upbeat, fun, good person, a nice person. I knew it as soon as he sat down across from me and I saw him smile. When he proposed, he said to me, "I love you for the person you are and the person you'll be."

advice for others
marriage is a partnership.

I think you have to look for someone who is going to be your partner. Who will work with you on things, be with you, and enjoy. It's very hard work. You're constantly compromising. It's not always going to be your way and not always going to be his way, and when you have a child it's neither of your ways. It's a huge amount of compromise. Pick your battles. Don't fight every battle. Don't swing at every pitch. We put up with a lot from each other. We've had some terrible fights. He watches a lot of television, which annoys me, and we have different ideas about what a "clean" apartment means. And there are obviously choices about money and working and sacrifice, what we can spend, what we can't spend. There's a lot of negotiating.

Everybody has his own craziness. It just has to be tolerable, and you have to be able to accept that fact. Don't marry someone just because he's fun. Look for someone who is reliable, predictable, will care for children, and has his act together.

love at first sight

The "love grumblers" among us can scoff that maybe love at first sight was more believable back in the days of men in stockings professing love to women on balconies. But in truth, those women on balconies (and stuck on desert islands) were doubters too.

In Shakespeare's *The Tempest,* Ferdinand, the Prince of Naples, declares to his beloved Miranda, "The very instant that I saw you, did my heart fly to your service." He might be a prince, but she's wary. Cognizant of that more common occurrence—lust at first sight—she asks him, "But do you love me?" "Honey," he assures her, "I do love, prize, and honor you."

And he does.

how rachel *met* rafael

Met: May 1997 in Washington, D.C. Both Rachel and Rafael were twenty-six.

Married: August 2000

I had just started a new job at a law firm as a recruiting assistant. We had about twenty-five new summer associates starting in a month—they had been hired before I started, so

I didn't know much about any of them. We had asked that they fill out a questionnaire and send a picture for our firm-wide newsletter to announce their arrival. I had a thing for Hispanic men, so I was particularly interested in getting the bio from an incoming summer associate named Rafael. When he finally sent in his information (late, by the way) I looked at the picture and thought he was very hot. Then I looked down at the info sheet and saw that his birthday was two days before mine. Right then, I thought it was destiny and that I would marry him.

A couple of other things went into my thinking this. For instance, our first names are two letters apart—and they're not common names, either (Rafael, Rachel). This was just like my parents' names, Josiah and Josie, and growing up I had always thought that my parents' names were so cool. Rafael had gotten his undergraduate degree from MIT, and I knew one day I wanted to move back to Boston to be closer to my family in Vermont.

The next weekend I was walking with my friend Maira to a party. I told her about Rafael, the coincidences, and my conclusions about marrying him. Seeing how we had just left my boyfriend's house and she was always hearing silly things come out of my mouth, she thought I was crazy.

When I met Rafael for the first time, he was a little shorter and skinnier than I'd imagined. (I'm six foot one and he's five ten.) A couple of days later, we were all out at a bar after the welcome dinner for the summer associates. We were drunk (me, more so) and I told him about some of the coincidences and hit on him. I knew I wasn't going to marry my current

oldest, highest, mostest

According to the 2006 edition of the *Guinness Book of World Records,* the world's oldest bride was Minnie Munro, who at the age of 102 married Dudley Reid, age 83, at Point Claire, Australia on May 31, 1991.

The countries with the highest marriage rate are Antigua and Barbuda, with 22.1 marriages per 1,000 people in 1998. (The U.S. marriage rate in 2000 was 8.4 marriages per 1,000 people.)

And one couple have renewed their marriage vows more times than any other. Lauren Lubeck Blair and David E. Hough Blair have married each other eighty-three times, most recently in Las Vegas on August 16, 2004.

---

boyfriend and I had a hunch about Rafael, even before we met. I felt like I had to go for it—so I seized the moment and didn't really think of the consequences.

Rafael couldn't really understand me because it was loud in the bar, but we ended up making out in the alley behind the restaurant. (He also had a girlfriend, but at the time neither of us knew that the other was dating someone else.) A couple of weeks later, his roommate was out to dinner with some friends. My then-boyfriend was at the other end of the table. Rafael's roommate mentioned that Rafael was hooking up with the recruiting assistant at firm X, and my then-boyfriend said, "Hey, my girlfriend is the recruiting assistant at Firm X." Washington, D.C., is a big city, but it turned very small that day. That night my boyfriend called me, told me what he had heard, and broke up with me.

Maira read a Spanish poem at our wedding three years later in Vermont. We moved to Boston three months after that and now, ten years later, we have two beautiful boys. I loved Rafael from almost the beginning and every year our marriage is better and better. I still believe it was all destiny. My husband thinks I am just plain crazy.

advice for others
don't waste time with the wrong one.

Listen to your inner voice and heart when it comes to finding the right one. I kept wondering if he was out there for me or if what I currently had (or had in the past) was all I could hope for. I really liked my boyfriends and they treated me like gold, but I always knew something was missing. I can remember being in the bathroom at a party I went to with one of my boyfriends pre-Raf and saying out loud in the mirror to myself, "I will never marry him." Once I met Raf, I knew he was the one, and I never looked back or ever questioned myself. I tell my girlfriends not to waste time with the wrong one. It is easy to get caught up in the daily routine and hard to break away from your comfort zone, but it's better to be alone than with the wrong guy.

You can't be passive about finding him, either. You can't sit in your apartment and say, "Oh, it will happen, if it's going to." If there was an opportunity for me to go to any kind of event and I really didn't feel like it, I would tell myself, "Tonight could be the night that you meet him." It didn't happen for me that way, but if you sit on your couch it's 100 percent guaranteed not going to happen.

how james *met* sarah

Met: March 2002 in Washington, D.C. James was thirty-three and Sarah was twenty-five.

Married: June 2004

I had just returned to Washington, D.C., from a business trip in Florida and had lost my cell phone charger. My producer said she would leave it with the concierge at the Ritz Carlton Hotel, so I stopped there on the way back from the airport.

I had fallen asleep on the plane and my hair was a mess, and I was wearing a parka over my suit. I didn't look my best. I could have been in and out of the Ritz in thirty seconds, but then I laid eyes on this strikingly beautiful woman dressed in a formal evening gown. She was seated alone on the couch. I stopped and caught my breath for a second. I thought instantly of going over to talk to her. (This was smack in the middle of my boldest single days.) But then I realized that she was obviously at the hotel to attend some formal event and thus probably had a date somewhere. Knowing my luck, he would reappear precisely when I hit my stride—and he'd look like George Clooney. I didn't need that kind of embarrassment and humiliation. But I couldn't walk away from her, either.

So I actually sat down on a couch across the lobby and stole glances through the willow-bud decorative shrub on the table between us. Later she told me that number one, she had said to herself, "I bet he's a reporter" (which I am); number two, "I wonder what it would be like to be married to someone like that"; and number three, "He's staring at me, and isn't it cute that he doesn't seem to have the nerve to come over and talk to me?"

I finally decided that I couldn't chance the reappearance of George Clooney but I couldn't let her go altogether, either. So I decided to do something that struck me as a happy medium. I walked over to her, made a courtly little bow, and in one fluid motion produced my business card from my shirt pocket, handed it to her, nodded and walked away without speaking. The entire transaction was conducted without words. About five paces away, exiting the room, I looked back over my shoulder. She was smiling at me.

attraction at first sight

"Love is an in-depth phenomenon. It's really impossible to love another person you don't know. What is possible is attraction at first sight. If you are lucky, that translates over time to love. When people remember, 'The first time I saw him, I fell in love,' they mean they were attracted. If it doesn't become love, you remember you were attracted, not in love, at first sight. And a little while later it's, 'What was I thinking?'"
—Scott R. Wersinger, PhD, professor of biophysiological human psychology at the State University of New York at Buffalo

I met friends for drinks and I told my best friend, "I have just handed my card to the most gorgeous, hottest woman I have ever seen in my life." And my friend responded, "Why are you even bothering to tell us about this? You're never going to see her again."

The next day I went on a twelve-country, ten-day trip to the Middle East. When I was in Amman, Jordan, I checked my messages. In one of them, I heard a female voice saying, "Hi James, this is Sarah. We met at the Larry King Cardiac Foundation Gala. I'm sorry it's taken me so long to get back to you. Here's my number." I hadn't attended the Larry King Cardiac Foundation Gala. My first thought was, "Some bastard's been handing out my business cards. I better go and stop him." When I got back home, I Googled the term "Larry King Cardiac Foundation Gala 2002" and up came "Ritz Carlton." I thought to myself: "Oh! The Ritz Carlton lady!"

For no other reason than to be a bastard, when I called Sarah back I played dumb. I said, "Sarah? This is James. I'm sorry it's taken me so long to get back to you, but I've been traveling in the Middle East"—subtext: I'm important, compelling, and handsome—"and I must say I've never been to the Larry King Cardiac Foundation Gala." She said, "We met in the hallway." I dropped my voice down an octave and said, "Are you the lovely young lady who was seated alone on the couch in formal wear?" I could hear her eyes rolling over the phone. She said "Yes" with impatience. I dropped down an octave lower still and said, "I'm very glad you called." No cheesy stone left unturned. It's amazing she even went out with me.

Thereafter, whenever we went to the Ritz Carlton I would make her reenact the scene of our meeting. One time she sat in the chair and I sat across from her and sidled up to her and I threw my card at her. On another occasion, I sidled up to her and I dropped forty-six cards on her, Woody Allen–style.

I proposed there too. I sidled up and produced—the ring.

advice for others
expect it when you least expect it—and in the meantime, keep the faith.

Although I always imagined I would marry a smart, beautiful, and compassionate woman—and Sarah is all of those things, in spades—she is otherwise very different from the particular kind of woman with whom I thought I would wind up spending my life. I was, and remain, immersed in the classic Washington, D.C., experience: politics, media, the law. And yet I married a woman who is a true civilian by capital-city standards. The lesson I draw is to keep an open mind, welcome new people and experiences, and abide by the John Lennon dictum that life is what happens to one when one is engaged in the making of altogether different plans.

how kate *met* leonard

Met: September 2003 in Washington, D.C. Kate was twenty-three and Leonard was twenty-six.

Married: October 2005

After I graduated from college, I worked for a national crime-prevention organization as the only full-time staff member in the busy Washington, D.C., office. They sent me to a conference in California to pitch administrators on a program to get college students involved with safety by mobilizing them based on what they saw as problems on their campuses. After the conference, I wrote follow-up letters to the administrators who had been at the conference saying, "Don't forget me. Call if you want to get started."

One of the people I met was chief of campus police at a university in Washington, D.C. When I got back from the conference, I received an e-mail from Leonard, who was the university's crime prevention officer. We set up a time to meet. His name—first and last—his tone and his writing all led me to believe he was around fifty years old. I went in thinking he was a rough-around-the-edges, older, gruff kind of person. He later told me because of the tone of my voice on the phone, he thought I was older too.

The day I planned to meet him, I was also meeting interns to try to convince them to come work with me. I was lugging this big suitcase around with me—I was not graceful. But I had on a suit and heels and a sexy pushup bra, so I was looking and feeling gorgeous. I wheeled the awkward suitcase into the campus department of safety. It was my first site visit, so I was really nervous. They paged Leonard to come upstairs, and he came in.

I took one look and just turned bright red. I don't know if anybody swoons in this day and age, but I felt like swooning. Something just snapped in me. He was tall and gorgeous and around my age. I remember one of the first thoughts I had was, "We'd make cute babies," which was premature, but I couldn't help it. On the way to his office, he offered to carry my big suitcase. I said, "No, no, no, I'll do it," so there I was in my heels lugging this giant thing down a flight of stairs.

After we talked for about twenty minutes, he agreed to go ahead with the program. Then we talked for another hour, about family and where we were from, and we discovered a friendly rivalry between the Ducks and the Wolverines, the Oregon and Michigan football teams. They were playing each other, which they don't do often. When I left, I called my mom and my best friend and said, "I met somebody."

I knew he was in a relationship—that came out in our hour of chatting—and I had a boyfriend, too, so I wasn't sure where it would go. I just felt different. I knew that this was

marriage in biblical times | In the Book of Genesis, first cousins married. (After all, there weren't that many people around.)

late great loves

"He met his wife at the Silver Roller skating club of Silver Spring, Maryland and they became a roller-skating team. After they won first prize in a fancy skating contest in 1935, they became professional skaters. They performed 'Death on Wheels' on the carnival circuit and were in the cast of the third 'Going Native Revue' at Loews Fox Theater in Washington. They were known in news stories as 'two of Washington's best fancy skaters,' and they performed until 1941."
—From the obituary of Stephen Joseph Hunter, the *Washington Post,* February 8, 2007

a special connection because I had been there, sitting in his office, talking myself out of my current boyfriend.

Leonard and I were supposed to have monthly conference calls to get the crime-prevention program going. He invited me to watch the Oregon-Michigan game, but I had a board meeting and had to turn him down. It was months before we talked again. He wasn't available for conference calls, he didn't return e-mails—he dropped off the face of the earth.

Finally, after three months, he instant messaged me to explain that right after we met, he had gotten hit in the face with a softball and had to have reconstructive facial surgery on his eye socket and jaw. I remember thinking, "Oh no!" because I wasn't sure what had happened to his face!

He had broken up with his girlfriend, and we started chatting online. However, I still had a boyfriend. This time was like a gray area when we knew something would happen but didn't know how. We chatted online nonstop; I felt like I was

dream come true

The love and marriage we—literally—dream of might actually be en route. According to The Encyclopedia of Dream Interpretation, dreams of compact discs, bedroom, mares, or flight don't mean a friend still hasn't returned your music, you are aware you are in bed, you just saw a Western or freedom. Instead:

- Compact Disc: "A dream about a CD implies that the dreamer will soon become involved in a new romantic liaison that will go very well."
- Bedroom: "If a single person has this dream, the dream implies that he will get married sooner than expected. Even if a wedding is not yet in the offing (and even if there is no partner in evidence), the dream implies that he will get married much more quickly than he thought."
- Mare: "If a young woman dreams about a mare, it means that she will have a good marriage and lovely children."
- Flying: "A dream about flying with white wings over green vegetation means success in business and love."

in junior high. We finally set a date to meet at a local bar, and I definitely wore that pushup bra again. After the date, I broke up with my boyfriend. By the second date, I just knew Leonard was for me.

Len says he fell in love with me on that second date. He joined my friends and me for a before-Thanksgiving party. He must have liked the way I make mashed potatoes. Two years later, he proposed the day after Thanksgiving while we were iceskating. I definitely wasn't expecting it; it actually felt too soon. But I knew in my heart that he was the one for me, so I said yes.

advice for others
trust your instincts.

My mother told me two things. One was right, and one was wrong: "You are going to meet the friend of a friend" and "You'll just know." I didn't meet the friend of a friend. But I did just know. I had no idea what that meant until I met Leonard. I think what my mom meant was to trust myself. You have to trust your instincts on love. When we're young, our brains are superactive. We overthink everything. The choice of a husband, for me, was simple. My relationship with Leonard is the one thing I never overthink. With everything else, I'm hard-pressed to make a decision. I still can't pick a career, a degree program, a paint color, a shampoo. If I do pick, I'm always left with doubt. But I never doubted him—even though I feel like I'm still getting to know him—and each time we fight, I'm annoyed, or we aren't mixing, I find peace in trusting myself. There is something bigger than this current worry. I instinctively loved this man; I made my choice, and I was right.

not exactly love at first sight

*H*e's supposed to make her heart race, not her eyes roll. I agree with Elie Wiesel, who said that the opposite of love isn't hate, it's indifference. These couples prove it—love is pretty close to hate. Close enough to want to kick and kiss him, in some cases. And sometimes it's not capital-H Hate, it's "Your-blonde-friend-is-cute-sorry-I-forgot-your-name" hate, which, when you're on the receiving end of it, smarts too. Sometimes what looks like repulsion is actually passion (stay with me here). Something about the way she makes him feel is so unusual, it's uncomfortable. The way he ruins your concentration is maddening. Yes, sometimes hate is hate. But sometimes, as Amanda likes to say, it's "love at first fight."

how amanda *met* michael

Met: August 2005 in Austin, Texas. Amanda was twenty and Michael was thirty.

Married: January 2006

I was studying to be a pastry chef at Texas Culinary Academy, and on my first day I sat next to him. We had to pair up and make pineapple upside-down cake—I hate pineapple upside-down cake—and I asked him if I could be his partner. I thought Michael was cute. He has crystal-clear blue eyes that would make any girl weak in the knees, but once he opened his mouth I reconsidered. He said to me, "I work alone."

I thought, "Who the hell does he think he is?" He pissed me off, so I said, "I'm going to get the ingredients." Since he made me angry, I took it upon myself to ruin his day. He later told me he thought, "Who the hell are you to be good enough to be my partner?" Of course I knocked him down off that pedestal.

I'd put salt in his sugar. He'd move my stuff to where I couldn't find it, or he'd pull my chair back so I'd fall when

don't i know you from somewhere?

Julia Ingram, co-author of *The Messengers: A True Story of Angelic Presence and a Return to the Age of Miracles,* is a psychotherapist, hypnotherapist, and master past-life regression therapist. In an essay on her website, *www. juliaingram.com,* she recounts the case of "two people who met at a party and within one hour felt that they needed to divorce their respective spouses in order to be together." After a past-life regression therapy session, it was discovered that during the Revolutionary War he had been a wounded young soldier and she a Native American who saved him. On the woman's deathbed, the two had agreed to be together forever. Ingram explained to them that, "pledges made in other lifetimes, especially at death, can seem like contracts that must be kept. But I pointed out that it was not so." Strong immediate feelings—whether loving or hateful "are a clue as to a possible past-life origin," she says.

I went back to sit. I don't like just rolling out of bed so I'd take the time to put on makeup before class; he'd ask if I was going somewhere after class. I hated him; he got under my skin. He was just so cocky, and it was a complete turnoff.

We were totally at each other's throats for a whole month. But even though we were mean to each other in class, I would look in his eyes and flirt a little. I would joke around that maybe we would get locked in the cooler together. Sometimes he would say, "Well maybe I'll just drag you in there," and other times he would ignore me. But when it came to whose dessert was better, he could get really mean. If I was lucky, I would get an "It's okay" from him about my creations. His was always better—well, except for the one where I switched some of his sugar with salt.

I guess you could say we could get pretty dramatic when it came to our desserts. I'd unplug his mixer and he'd take a half hour to figure it out. He'd say, "Yours tastes terrible" and he'd stomp around and make a face and not talk to me. Once I put vinegar in one of his desserts. It came out much better and he took total credit: "It came to me in a vision."

When my grades started getting close to his, he started to think I was worthy. He flirted more with me. He started asking me out for coffee. I would say, "Why would I want to do that?" I stood him up a good twenty times, yet he was so persistent. When I missed class one day, I asked him for notes. He walked me to my door and grabbed me and kissed me. I was thinking, "Oh my God, he's kissing me. I hate this guy!" I was in total shock. I had always been physically attracted to him but just couldn't get past his bad attitude. Even with the slight flirting in class, no one could have predicted that he'd be grabbing me out of nowhere to kiss me. I just stood there. He said, "Are you going to let me in?" I moved aside so he could come in but I was speechless for a good thirty minutes.

I found out I was pregnant shortly after we started dating. Michael was doing a cake competition in Tulsa, Oklahoma, at the time and I called to tell him the shocking news. I said, "There's a bun in the oven," and he said, "Well, I'll wait while you get it out of the oven."

"No, Michael, I mean there's a *bun* in the *oven.*" Of course there was silence, as I had expected. When he came home and the pregnancy test came out with those pretty blue lines, he turned beet red. He started hugging me and kissing me to the point where I could barely breathe.

He had asked me three or four times to marry him, and I'd said no. He had the nerve to ask me the first time over a text message when he was sitting right next to me. I was so mad, I said, "If you are going to ask me, do it nicely. Don't be cocky and do it over a text message." I got up and left.

Now we're married and own a catering company together. When we bake, the hate side of our love-hate relationship comes right out. Usually he wants to make things more complicated, or we don't see eye-to-eye on the end product, and we immediately start arguing. Don't ask me how, but even with all the yelling and the throwing of scrap pieces of pastries at each other it works.

We make each other try different things. I introduced him to different designs and styles, like bright colors—he likes them now, instead of the earthy ones. He makes me eat things I don't want to eat. He made me eat snails. I cringed the first time but ended up loving them.

We're like cake and icing. Some people like plain cake. Personally, I like eating icing; he likes the cake. Together it's this wonderful concoction. It was never love at first sight. More like love at first fight. It puts a nice kick into the relationship.

advice for others
take a taste.

It's like going to a fancy restaurant and seeing food that seems disgusting and smells horrible. But he was so unexpected and delightful, like the snails. I could not have eaten anything else for the rest of my life. It was that great.

how robert *met* maryann

Met: November 1967 in the Bronx, New York. Both Robert and Maryann were twenty.

Married: December 1969

It was a warm fall Sunday night and as typical of our youth back in the sixties, I was cruising the neighborhood in my "White Knight," a Chevy Supersport, with the windows down. My younger friend Ritchie was riding shotgun.

We had cruised the standard avenues of the Bronx seeking the fantasy pickup that never really happened. I announced that I had enough for one night and headed home to mentally prepare myself for another week of school and work. Driving south on the Grand Concourse, near the Paradise Theatre, we saw the unbelievable. Two gals were walking north toward us. Hoping that the evening would still bring surprises, Ritchie called out and said hello to the girls. Even though we were passing at a high rate of speed, I noticed one of the young ladies had striking long blonde hair. To our shock, they responded with a wave and hello.

Unfortunately, with traffic behind me on the busy thoroughfare, I couldn't stop before traveling another few blocks. By now, the girls were out of sight and probably disappearing into the busiest intersection in the Bronx, Fordham Road and the Grand Concourse. Faced with failure, I did what any other hormone-induced youth would do. I pulled a U-turn across six lanes of traffic and circled back toward Alexander's department store.

Sure enough, up ahead we saw the blonde and her friend. We stopped the car and asked them a few questions. After some small talk they happily accepted our offer to drive up to a meeting spot in Yonkers for a cup of coffee. They introduced themselves. The blonde was Rosemarie, and the other girl was Maryann.

After the typical dialog, we discovered that they were college students at Bronx Community and we had several mutual acquaintances. In fact, sitting at the table across from us were some guys they had met the same way a few weeks earlier.

quote/ unquote	"He thought I was aloof and I thought he was arrogant. It just shows you how wrong you can be. But once he kissed me that was that." —Actress Cate Blanchett on her husband, screenwriter Andrew Upton

We decided it was getting late and since there didn't seem to be any "magic" in the conversation, I offered to drive them home.

At the time I was unaware that the two girls had secretly given each other the signal that neither one of them had any interest in Ritchie or me. If either of us asked for a telephone number, they would give us a false one. We dropped Maryann off first; she told us that Rosemarie would provide us with their numbers. After a short drive, we came to Rosemarie's apartment house, where we asked her for their telephone numbers. Later, I was informed that Rosemarie hadn't been concentrating. It was only by mistake that she gave us the real numbers.

With the memory of Rosemarie's long blonde hair and tight jeans, I called her. She seemed very aloof. I tried a second call a few days later and got the same result. I threw out her number. After a few weeks, I couldn't even remember their names. Finally, with nothing happening during a holiday break in classes, I asked Ritchie if he had the number for the other girl—the skinny one. He searched and searched. He found the matchbook in the bottom of his junk drawer with the number scrawled on the inside cover. Amazingly, he had not used up the matches or discarded them somewhere.

I called Maryann, but her mother said she was unavailable. A few days later, after a lengthy conversation with her mother, I got the same result. Now, with rejection and total failure within reach, I was determined to speak with her, whatever her name was. Her mother answered again. But this time, Mom told Maryann to at least speak to me. She did. We talked. And we talked. Forty years later, we are still talking.

I'm such a believer in fate. Even today, when talking about that first night when we met, we still wonder to each other, "What if I had gotten stuck at a red light?"

advice for others
laugh and emulate the willow tree.

The big thing that has kept us really happy is a sense of humor. We both like to laugh and have fun. We both like each other's company, and we're best friends. We have never had a serious fight. Yeah, sure, there are disagreements, but we've never gone more than a few hours being mad at each other. Sense of humor has been critical. We also enjoy each other's company and are respectful and understanding of each other's feelings. On my part, I'm more bending. I'm almost like a willow, rather than an oak that snaps in the wind. There's give and take.

how lauren *met* andrew

Met: February 1998 in Amherst, Massachusetts. Lauren was twenty and Andrew was twenty-one.

Married: October 2003

Andrew and I lived in the same dorm our junior year at Amherst. I thought he was a big scary guy. He *is* a big guy—six foot three—and he can be very quiet, which can come off as angry. I was friends with his group of friends, his baseball teammates, but not with him. I remember sitting talking with them while he just sat in his chair. I felt like he was totally ignoring me. The vibe was grumpy and intimidating. He thought I was stuckup because I talked to his friends and not to him. At the same time, he says that the first time he saw me walking across the field with my ponytail bobbing, he thought, "She's very beautiful." But he had a girlfriend at the time.

About a week after Valentine's Day, there was a party in one of the dorm suites. Andrew had shaved his head and was bald as a baby. I had had a few drinks, and he apparently had a lot to drink. I went up to him and said, "Can I rub your head?" He said, "Sure." He was off his rocker. The next thing I know, we were talking and even hugging at one point. Then we were sitting and chatting, I couldn't tell you about what. I was thinking, "This is a guy I don't know or like and I'm hugging him and rubbing his head." All of a sudden he got very quiet and looked down and he put his hands in his lap. I said, "Are you okay?" and he said, "I don't feel very good."

I said, "Do you want to go to bed?" And he said "Yeah." So I walked him back to his room and helped him get his shoes off and went on my merry way. The next day, I thought, "I really enjoyed talking to him and I should see how he's doing." So I made up an excuse to go past his window to see if he was in. He was, so I went up and checked on him. His side of the dorm was closest to the library and I lived on the side farthest away from the library. Needless to say, the next week I went to the library a lot.

For some reason I thought he liked Blow Pops, those hard lollipops with the gum inside. I used to buy them and say, "I thought you might like these." He couldn't figure out why I kept buying him Blow Pops but he'd say, "Oh, great," when I gave them to him. After a few weeks of getting to know each other, we ended up sitting in his room one night and talking until four in the morning.

Within about two months, I remember thinking I loved him and being totally freaked out about that because I had

late great loves

"Shy and modest to a fault, he met his wife-to-be during a visit to the Bronx Zoo. The young woman realized there was more to this introverted scientist and engineer than she initially thought when he happened to comment, 'Elephants have kind eyes.' She told herself, 'I'm going to marry this guy.' She did, in 1949."
—From the obituary of Eric Wolf, *Washington Post,* April 20, 2007

come out of an awful long-term relationship. No one knew about us until pretty much the last day of school. We kept it very under the radar. But within a few weeks I was thinking, "This guy is really special." I wasn't looking for anybody. I had been single for nine months, and it was great. And I was only twenty or twenty-one when we got together.

A few weeks, maybe a month after we started dating, I got really sick with the stomach flu. I remember thinking, "I have to find Andrew," which is a bizarre reaction. Nothing is hotter than taking care of a sick girl! But he came over and took care of me.

I told Andrew from the very beginning that I didn't want to get married. He didn't care either way. Then a friend of his from the college baseball team died in the September 11th attack on the Twin Towers. He and his wife had been married only thirty days. I realized that a part of me wanted that kind of public affirmation of our relationship. Andrew was fine either way; he just waited to see what I wanted to do. Finally I said, "Okay, I'm ready to get married."

advice for others
let go of preconceived notions.

I always tell my little sister that I didn't go looking for anything, and I just let things happen. We didn't start with preconceived notions, "This has to go to marriage" or a certain way. We were just open to where the relationship went and open to each other. We've gone through all sorts of difficult things and lived in different places and changed our minds about our careers, but we've both been willing to support the other person completely without losing ourselves. I think that has been the most important thing. Be open. Go with the flow. We never had a conversation about being together. I know that doesn't work for everybody, but it worked for us. We said, "Let's just do it."

how lew *met* catherine

Met: Summer of 1983 in New Buffalo, Michigan. Lew was thirty-eight, Catherine was twenty-six.

Married: October 1984

Friends introduced me to Catherine when were both hanging out on their boat—and she didn't seem the least interested in talking to me. It wasn't until later that I learned she thought I was still dating a girl I had actually just broken up with. At the time, I decided Catherine was a cold fish and thought, "I'll just scratch her off my list."

The second time I met her, later that summer, I was on my boat and our mutual friends were anchored off a beach in Lake Michigan and I swam over. I had had a couple beers, I swam underwater and came up and pinched her butt as she floated there in the inner tube. She didn't think much of that, and I didn't really care.

Not long after, I got transferred back east. We were 700 miles apart. Around March, one of these mutual friends said,

"Catherine will be in Atlantic City. Take her out to dinner." But it was a two-hour ride to get there. I called her Monday night and said, "Yeah, hi, I'm not driving all the way to Atlantic City just for dinner." We ended up talking for about an hour, a good conversation, and suddenly she didn't seem like a cold fish anymore. I thought, "Well, heck, maybe it would be worthwhile to go to see her." So I drove out there—in the snow.

We had a good first date and saw each other in a different light after that. I even spent the weekend with her. I had decided I was going to go back to Michigan to get my boat loaded on a truck to bring it east and I asked her, "Why don't you come back east and sail with me on the Chesapeake?" Soon she was coming down every other week to go sailing. She was really good on the boat.

I had had long-distance relationships before, and I knew it was hard to keep them going. I decided to not worry about it and just see the relationship as a summer fling. But when her job offered to send her for her MBA, she had to make a decision. She told me, "Either I'm going to stop coming or you're going to make a commitment." I said, "Oh, I hadn't been thinking that." I hadn't even considered a serious commitment. So I said, "Come back next weekend and I'll give you the answer."

If Catherine had decided we were a good match and she was ready to commit to me, I had to rethink the whole situation. I thought we were interacting well, having a good time, and I thought we probably would be a good match. She came back the next week and I said, "Okay, I'm ready." Once I made the decision, I had no qualms about it whatsoever.

It was like a switch went off. Before, I was in a real quandary—"What should I do?" But I made the decision and I'm happy about it, so let's go, let's move on. I never looked back. It's been good. I feel lucky she forced me to make a decision.

I had been in at least three long-term relationships. I never felt anxious to get married. I told Catherine that I knew when I was five years old I never wanted to get married—I don't know why. But I can remember my mom saying something that started with the statement, "When Lew gets married," and I said, "I'm not getting married." By the time I met Catherine I was thirty-eight and a happy confirmed bachelor. I had my toys, and I was having fun. I didn't want to have kids; I wasn't interested. I was already thinking, "It's safe to say I'm never going to get married."

We are a good fit, a good match. Our strengths and weaknesses complement each other. Of all the women I had dated, she is the best match for me.

advice for others
opposites work and the past opens doors.

We're totally opposite, and we work because of it. I do a lot of team facilitating and coaching, and I really value people's strengths. I'm used to thinking in those terms. I tend to be the one who straightens up, while Catherine can get things done very quickly but leaves a mess behind. I clean it up. I don't get mad. I say, "That's my job." She's a thinking person, and I'm an intuitive/feeling person, which is kind of a role-reversal for men and women. We lived on the boat for almost year and

| quote/ unquote | Groucho Marx: "How did you meet your wife?"
Man: "A friend of mine."
Groucho: "Do you still regard him as a friend?" |

took it to the Bahamas—and the key to making it work in close proximity, so you're not in conflict and not overlapping, is to clearly know who is responsible for what.

After having been through many relationships and being disappointed when they ended, I can see that in retrospect, it was good that they ended. What came later and last was the best thing for me. As one door closes, another door opens. I now view earlier relationships as developmental to help me grow into a better person and that qualified me to be the right person for the final relationship that I'm gratefully in.

chapter 6

relationship redux

Sometimes you're just not ready the first time. Sometimes you've got some growing up to do and she's got some wild oats to sow. Sometimes, even after you've put him through hell, he still takes you back. The stories of these couples run the gamut. But I noticed a common thread: maturity. Beth wasn't ready to act married when she was in college, so she split with clingy Bob.

Anna didn't think she could be the intellectual Bob needed, so she let him go. In the end, the couples reunited. Anna and Bob . . . well, their redux took a little longer than usual, but they led rich lives apart and also ended up where they should be—together.

how beth *met* bob

Met: September 1985 in Ithaca, New York. Both Beth and Bob were sixteen.

Married: July 1998

We both grew up in Ithaca and met in high school because his girlfriend's locker was next to mine—her last name was Murphy and mine was Moon. He was very nerdy, and I hung around with lots of different kinds of people. Then we both went to Cornell and just by chance we were next-door neighbors in the dorm. We were best friends during our freshman and sophomore years. He really wanted to date me, but I was dating his best friend. Then in our junior year we decided to go on a date. We saw a movie and had a nice dinner. We went for a long walk and made out under a moonlit sky in a field—he's a romantic guy. We started dating, but he was very clingy; he wanted to be a married couple, and I wasn't into that. I broke up with him in spring of that year. He was devastated. I was upset too. I also worked for his mother, which was a little awkward.

We didn't talk for six years. I went on with my life. He went to Los Angeles to start his own life. I dated a few other people and even lived with a guy for two years. (I broke up with him when he told me that if he married at all, he wanted to be married to several people at once.)

We had both been invited to the same two weddings—one in the fall and the other in the spring, so I knew we were going to have to see each other. I e-mailed him to clear the air so it wouldn't be uncomfortable for our friends. He was happy to hear from me, which was shocking. We had a nice little e-mail relationship and at the first wedding, in the spring of 1996, we held hands. After the wedding, Bob and I started talking on the phone.

At the second wedding, that fall, he picked me up at the airport with roses. We decided to start dating—though my mom didn't want me to get back together with him because she didn't want me to move to California!

He told me that in college I had been cold. Which is probably true. I wasn't ready for that level of relationship. But now that I was older, I was more interested in taking it to the next level. I also noticed that he got more mature and less clingy.

While we were in college, one of the things that had turned me off most was that he had been accepted into a writing program at the University of Southern California in the summer of our junior year but he didn't want to go because he would miss me. He ended up moving to Los Angeles in part because he was pissed at me for breaking up with him. He met his business partner there, and he knew some guys at Disney. They sold Disney a script and they've been there ever since. If I hadn't broken up with him, we'd be living in Ithaca. He'd be working at a bank, and we'd be divorced and miserable. Instead, we grew together apart.

advice for others
lots of advice for others.

There are lots of things I would advise other people to do:

- Stick with the nerds. Guys who are popular in high school peak early and fizzle out.
- On our honeymoon, we went to a luau that was full of married people and honeymooners. The host was cheesy; he asked the couple who had been married the longest their secret and they said, "Never go to bed angry." My grandparents say that, too.
- We tease quite often and don't let each other get away with anything, but in a gentle way. Take your mate and relationship

seriously and yourself not so seriously. Our first approach is humor, as opposed to starting off with anger. And when that doesn't work, we really let it fly!

• Having been apart, we both feel very lucky the other is back. We leave the house each morning with a routine. If it were the last time we ever saw each other, if one of us got hit by a bus, we'd want to be sure we've said goodbye in a way we wouldn't regret.

• If you don't want to create other people who behave (and look) just like the person you're considering for marriage, than the guy you are dating isn't the one. I want my kids to be just like my husband in most ways (maybe a little less hairy, but I can live with that), and I'm thrilled that they are turning out that way.

how claudia *met* mark

Met: October 1985 in Queens, New York. Claudia and Mark were both sixteen.

Married: March 1993

I was in high school and friends with Mark's sister. Mark and I met at a party I went to with her. The first time he and I got together we dated for a month, then he broke up with me. We continued to run into each other at parties and on college breaks, and we always ended up drunk and fooling around. After hooking up, he'd call me and we would go out again, but when I was sober I always realized I wasn't really that interested in him.

But it kept on happening—I'd see him again, and the same thing would happen. It was a vicious cycle that I couldn't break.

He was a party guy; he liked to drink. I thought he was sexually aggressive. I knew I liked him, but I wasn't ready to have sex when I was nineteen or twenty. I would wonder, "Why am I with this guy who's pressuring me? This isn't going to happen." The last time we got together we had both finished our undergrad degrees. I sent him a birthday card—his birthday is one day before mine—and he called me and asked me out.

We dated for close to two months—regular, steady, every week. We went out every Thursday night but we weren't physical. The most he would do was shake my hand.

We later discussed why the last one actually stuck. He said that he had realized what he had been doing and he didn't want to scare me away again. So he took it really slow. And while he was taking it slow, I was thinking, "He doesn't like me anymore, he has a girlfriend, or he's gay—somewhere along the way, something went wrong." All the other times he had been very, very, very interested in sex. We were dating regularly, but there was no contact whatsoever. And I was thinking, "What's going on? What happened here? It's from one side of the spectrum to the other!"

We became friends, and we got along really well. We would talk anywhere and everywhere. We went to a lot of plays—and we'd talk all through the play. We got stuck in a bathroom once and were talking and talking the whole time. I knew we really connected. It wasn't just a physical thing. I really enjoyed spending time with him—and talking to him.

I had finally told myself, "Well, I like him enough that we can be friends." He waited another two months before he made a move. Then I knew: He likes me, and I like him.

advice for others
communicate.

The reason we're together is communication. We've been married for fourteen years, and we have three kids. It's hard to connect. Sometimes we sit down and talk and say, "Oh! This is why we got married—we like talking to each other." Being attracted and all that other stuff is important, sure, but if we didn't have communication, we'd have split a long time ago. There's always stuff going on. Sometimes I keep everything inside and then blow up; he'll look at me and say, "What's wrong? What's wrong?" Whatever I was keeping to myself turns out to be dumb or minor most of the time, and I realize it once we talk things out. He gets it out of me.

Even if the problem's minor, even if it's nagging, better to get it out than keep it in and wait until it becomes a bomb: "How come you turned your face when I went to kiss you?" "I don't know—I think I'm coming down with a cold." Communication: That's why we're together.

how denise *met* rich

Met: October 1992 in South Orange, New Jersey. Denise was twenty-one and Rich was nineteen.

Married: May 2007

I met Rich through one of my sorority sisters in college—he was her brother, actually. I thought he was pretty cute then, but he's younger than I am, and that matters when you're in college. I couldn't date my friend's little brother! I dated a friend of his, so I did end up spending a lot of time with him. At best, we had a lot of fun college memories, but he definitely didn't pay me any mind back then. I found myself wondering once what one of his girlfriends had that I didn't, but it was such a strange and random thought that I just ignored it.

My friendship with his sister picked up again a year after college, when I moved to her town in New Jersey. Since I was far from home, I spent a lot of time with her and her family. They were my family away from home, and I loved the closeness they all shared. Her brother, however, was a mystery. He was always upstairs in his room, a brooding guy in his twenties, too good to hang out with the family—let alone acknowledge me. For some reason, though, he intrigued me. I continued to ignore these thoughts and tried hard not to notice how nicely he was filling out from working out at the gym so much.

The family planned a trip out to Walt Disney World and invited me to come along. It was at a vacation-planning party that Rich and I really started talking. I found myself wanting to spend more time with him when the party was over. Soon after, he told his sister he liked me and wanted to know if it was okay to date me. She decided to help him out by pleading his case to me. I said no at first because of how close I was with their family. But I eventually relented and said we'd see what happened on the trip. Well, fireworks flew—and not just at the Magic Kingdom. We started dating immediately after that.

I wish I could say we lived happily ever after, but we were in our twenties. He was still more interested in going out with his friends and getting a house at the beach for the summer. In other words, I was cramping his style, so he broke things off. I was devastated—for a long time. It didn't make it any easier that I had to see Rich every time I went to visit his parents.

A year and a half later, we hit it off again at a big family party. Sparks flew even more intensely this time. My wish had come true—or so I thought. It lasted almost a year (off and on), but our attempts to keep our relationship quiet to his family until it became serious actually caused a lot of problems. I was tired of hiding, and it was pretty clear that he still didn't want to get very serious or settle down. I decided I couldn't take it any more and told him I wanted to find someone who wanted the same things that I did. He wanted me to be happy and let me go. I found what I was looking for in someone else not long after that.

Six months later, Rich came back to tell me he'd made a mistake. He loved me, he said, and he wanted to settle down and get married. I could see how sincere he was, and he made every effort to win me back. In the end, though, I told him I was happy with the guy I was dating and it was just too late.

But fate would not allow us to stay apart. We kept running into each other in random places, and I could see he still felt the same each time I saw him. There was no doubt in my mind that he truly loved me, but I was happy.

Then, after more than two years together, the guy I was dating balked when it came to deciding where the relationship

the couple that splits together, stays together

California State University at Sacramento psychologist Nancy Kalish studied 1,000 re-connected romances and found that nearly 75 percent were together a decade later.

was going. I always chose to give the other guy more time, and Rich kept getting hurt—especially when I got engaged. To say I broke his heart is an understatement. But I started to question it more and more. That was the chink in the armor that eventually allowed Rich to get through to me.

After Rich and I were finally together, we both sensed there was something missing in the relationship, but neither of us could identify what it was. I was so destroyed that I ran to my old love for comfort.

It was such a selfish thing to do. I wasn't ready to start a new relationship. I was a complete mess. I knew I needed to spend some time alone to heal, and my knee-jerk reaction to run to my ex just ended up destroying Rich and making my pain much worse. I never wanted to hurt Rich, but I did. I thought ending it with him was the right thing for both of us. He didn't deserve to be with someone who couldn't love him. I couldn't love anyone then. He said he never wanted to see me again.

I spent the next several months alone. I had never been without a boyfriend for very long, and I always felt I needed one to be happy. I realized I couldn't find the right man to love me until I learned who I was. My life had always revolved around a guy—I had no idea who I was or what I wanted. So I decided to figure that out. Over the next two years, things started happening for me. I met new friends, I tried new things, and I traveled. I was having the time of my life. I soon realized that I was ready to find love again. I was finally happy just being me.

I reached out to Rich. To this very day, I don't quite know what made me do it. Something compelled me to send him an e-mail to apologize for what had happened between us the last time we were together, to let him know how important his friendship had been to me, and to let him know I wished him well. I was planning to move closer to my family in the coming year, and for some reason the thought of never seeing him again was haunting me.

Nausea washed over me when I hit the "Send" button. I didn't hear back from him that day or even in the next few days. I assumed that he didn't want to speak to me, but I had said what I'd wanted to say. I had closure . . . sort of.

Rich called me a few days later. My e-mail was torturing him and he had been trying hard not to call. He was starting to move on, and here I was again. His friends tried to physically stop him from calling, but he did it anyway. We went out for a couple of drinks a few days later, and I felt like a schoolgirl. I couldn't stop smiling and blushing.

We started dating again and found it wasn't easy to get past some of the pain we'd caused each other over the years. But we stuck it out, and one day we just fell back in love and knew that we completely trusted the love the other had for us. After nine years, we were finally at the same place at the same time. No more unrequited love.

advice for others
find yourself first.

After looking back at the whole situation and all the crazy things we put each other through, I wondered how we ended up together. Why did we go through all of that? Are we just crazy? I see now that we both had some growing to do on our own to get us to where we are now. I know those experiences on my own helped shaped who I am today, and I wouldn't trade them. I found myself through all of it, and then I was able to love the right man for me.

how bob *&* anna *met*

Met: September 1946 in Waco, Texas. Bob was seventeen and Anna was sixteen.

Married: May 2006

Anna: Bob and I were in high school at the same time. He was a couple of years ahead of me—we weren't together then. He was the football manager and I'd see him out on the field and in the hallways; I always thought he was a good-looking, red-headed boy. I was an usher at the Orpheum Theater and Bob would sit and watch me work.

Bob: I was supposed to be watching the movie.

Anna: I was in high school, and he had just graduated. He was the first boy I ever dated. I was pretty young and immature, but Bob was persistent and we dated some. We went on picnics whenever we could. He went off to college and I'd only see him when he came back to town. I went to one of the dances at Texas A&M University when he was in college. Our relationship kind of got serious for us to be so young. I felt like I would never get to go to college and Bob needed someone more his equal.

Bob: Anna was from a really poor family. This was right at the end of World War II and right after the Depression. Her father was not at home with the family, and her mother was raising two daughters and a son without an educated background. Anna made all her own clothes from the time she was twelve years old. She just knew she wasn't going to be able to afford—

Anna: I was forty-four when I went to college.

Bob: I think we're back to the breakup time, honey.

| **quote/ unquote** | "After all these years, I see that I was mistaken about Eve in the beginning; it is better to live outside the Garden with her than inside it without her."
—*Adam's Diary,* Mark Twain |

Anna: I think so, sweetie. I didn't ever think I'd ever have an educational background near his. So I broke it up.

Bob: We had started going together right after her sixteenth birthday; I was about seventeen. I was eighteen when we broke up. I was devastated. I was madly in love with her. I was trying to figure out a way to get married while still in college. I didn't have any money either. We didn't have any way to get married and make a home. She was wise in that regard. We [realized that we] couldn't be that serious and all.

Anna: We're from the old school, where we didn't have intimate relationships when we were young. We were close, and we knew that. We had to put some distance between us.

Bob: That just forced us apart. She told me to go away. I was devastated. It took me a long time to recover from that.

Anna: I knew it was a mistake. I kept hoping he'd come back.

Bob: I had my feelings hurt. My male ego.

Anna: I know, sweetie. We never saw each other again. I heard bits and pieces from a friend's husband who was at A&M. I heard when he married. I always regretted it and he was always in my heart. But life goes one. I had a family and he had a family. About twenty-five years ago, I saw him at his mother's funeral. I was single at that time. I used to spend the night with his mother when he was away at college. She was the sweetest little lady you ever saw. I had been married twenty-seven years and it ended in divorce. I didn't do anything—I didn't want to harm his marriage.

We didn't see each other again until March of 2006, when my youngest daughter decided to get us together again. I was four weeks out of surgery. My kids were encouraging me to get out. I was perfectly happy with my dog, but they thought I should go.

Bob: You swore off marriage.

Anna: I sure did.

Bob: And I did, too. I was five years widowed. When my wife died, I was retired—recently retired—and I was looking for things to do. I got really busy in the Presbyterian Church in Texarkana; I had been a member for years. I was by myself and started spending a lot of time in the church. I assumed I would finish my life a crotchety old man in church. Her daughter found out about me in a conversation with her mother and she called me. I got that phone call and my mind changed. I couldn't get back to her fast enough.

Anna: She said, 'Mom, we need to try to find him.' I said, 'Honey, he's married' and I wasn't going to bother him. My daughter said, 'At least let me find out, he may not be.'

Bob: Anna agreed to let her call Texarkana information and see if I was listed. She went ahead and called me.

Anna: She wasn't supposed to. She went behind my back. She asked for the lady of the house. He said, 'I'm a widower.'

Bob: And she said, 'In that case, do you remember Anna Huff?' And I said, 'Boy, do I remember Anna Huff.' She said, 'Mom's living alone and would like to talk to you. Would you mind if she called you some time?' I said, 'I'm old school—girls don't call the boys.' I asked for the number and called Anna myself.

Anna: It was wonderful. He sounded exactly like he had when he was young. One of the very first questions he asked me was, 'Do you still have that silver bathing suit?' I said, 'Sweetie, that would be rotten by now!' He said, 'Do you have a picture?' I happened to have one little snapshot.

Bob: We have that well framed. To remind us of the good old days. It was like we had never been apart. Almost like we had just had a date the night before.

quote/ unquote

"When Tracy did the show, I was involved with someone and she was living with someone. We worked together really well but didn't socialize or have deep, heart-to-heart talks. I really don't think either of us looked at each other romantically . . . But then, when I was doing *Bright Lights, Big City,* Tracy came in to audition and she was single and I was single, and ba-boom! It happened pretty quickly. We were engaged by that Christmas, weren't we?"
—Michael J. Fox on meeting his wife, Tracy Pollan, as quoted in *Redbook*

Anna: It was so natural. Not at all like sixty years. It was like coming home. Bob waited about three weeks and then he came to Waco to visit me. We only had a day and a half together. We needed that time for us and didn't tell my kids. My children were all up in the air—

Bob: I was a stranger to them.

Anna: So after Bob went back to Texarkana, we were on the phone continuously. All day, every day, and every night. So about five days after he went back, he accidentally asked me to marry him.

Bob: I of course wanted to spend more time together. We were working on how to get together. I said, 'There are many places I'd like to show you. Wait a minute we can't—we're not married.' I wasn't going to run around the country with her with her kids worrying. I thought about it a minute and I said, 'Anna, we'll have to get married.' And she said, 'Bob Street, are you proposing to me?' And I said, 'I guess I am.' And she said, 'In that case, I accept.'

Anna: Bob said, 'I don't want to be away from you another minute.'

Bob: That's right. My stepdaughter put it together in about a month.

Anna: A beautiful home wedding.

Bob: Scheduled around my minister's schedule. She's a lady. She had business—but she said, 'I can cancel a meeting,' and we had the wedding on May 6, 2006.

Anna: Back up just a little bit. Of course I called my children. My older daughter said, 'Momma, you can't marry a stranger. You don't even know this man.' I said, 'He's no stranger to me. I had a life before you were born.' So they called a family conference. They put him on the spot and asked him every kind of question. They weren't going to let me make a mistake.

Bob: I said, 'My feelings for Anna I can sum up: You take a great big dump truck. I've been filling it with love for her and it's running over. I'm going to put it in the driveway and dump it right over her.' They didn't ask any more questions.

Anna: They melted right away. They melted. I'm treated like a queen. I've never been so happy in my life. It feels so right.

Bob: Our first few months of marriage were difficult. About a month after our wedding date, I was found to have a recurrence of cancer in the bladder. Three weeks later, they discovered very serious heart problems and I had open-heart surgery. We were married less than two months. I've had four bypasses and a valve replaced. It was August before we could even move down to Waco.

Anna: I wouldn't let him travel. We've just started our honeymoon.

Bob: My wife had to take care of me. She's been wonderful.

Anna: He's easy. It's hard to explain, but I'm happier than I have ever been in my whole life.

Bob: I am working hard to make you happy!

Anna: You make me happy.

Bob: As you do me.

Anna: He hangs pictures of me and keeps hanging them. He says, 'I don't want you to be out of my sight.'

advice for others
cherish each other.

Anna: I think when you marry the right person, it's the most wonderful thing in the world. We marvel every day at our closeness. Every day is better than the day before. We tell each other every day. We take nothing for granted. We cherish each other tenderly.

Bob: Cherish means a lot to us—no eyes for anyone else or thoughts for anyone else. I think that's how marriage needs to be to work.

Anna: A lot of young couples think they have it, and later it goes sour. A lot of it is raising families and there is stress and compromise. You just have to love each other and tolerate and explore and work it out together.

Bob: I think a big mistake young people make is they both expect their mate to make them happy. A young lady says, 'Make me happy' and a man says the same. If they are thinking first that it's your job to make me happy, that is where they clash. If people put their mate's needs ahead of their own, the marriage works.

office meets

A whopping 58 percent of office workers admit they've had an office romance. Could be that there's something about the ethereal glow of the IT guy's face when he's right up close to your computer screen? Or maybe guys really do make passes at girls in glasses. It makes sense: If we spend eight or ten hours a day around our office mates, we're going to get to know them. And some of us are going to get to know each other really well. This chapter is about those for whom the term "endless meeting" took on a whole new meaning.

how doug *met* carolyn

Met: February 1969 in Indianapolis, Indiana. Doug was twenty-five and Carolyn was twenty-two.

Married: September 1969

We worked for the same company but were in different departments and had never met. I was a sales rep. When I made a sale, I would call in to input my order to a certain department. Many times I got this rep, Miss Flynn. She seemed like anybody else, a nice person. Then one day she had laryngitis. She had this cute squeaky voice, and I teased her about it.

After that, I was more interested in meeting her. We stayed on the phone only about five minutes, but her voice was so cute and when I teased her about it, she kinda laughed. I have no idea why; I just know that made me want to meet her. Before that we had talked maybe fifteen or twenty times. Most of the calls, all but one or two, were regular business transactions and might have taken ten or fifteen minutes.

The man who sat next to me said, "You ought to meet this girl." I found an excuse to go to her department, which was in another building, and introduce myself to her. I lived in this swinging singles building with way more men then women. Every Friday there was a party, a kegger. I invited Carolyn and she said yes. A little later I was talking to her on the phone and I said, "Do you want to just meet me there?" and she said, "Absolutely not." And I realized what a dummy I had been, so I made arrangements to pick her up.

I had only met her once. When I knocked on the door, her seventeen-year-old sister opened the door and I thought it was Carolyn. She had dark hair and the same complexion. I stumbled around a minute before Jane said, "Let me go get Carolyn for you."

At the party, I noticed that when she was talking to other guys, I didn't like it. That's when I first figured out I was really interested. From that day on, I had only one other date with another girl and that was because that date had already been scheduled. Carolyn and I became exclusive right away. I let her know, and she knew very early on, that I thought this was something really special. We met in February and got engaged in April and got married at the end of September.

Though the people in her department knew it, we kept the fact that we were dating a secret from other people in my department; we were afraid people wouldn't like it if we were dating. Another man in my department said, "There's a girl you oughta meet," and it was Carolyn. And we had just gotten engaged the weekend before!

advice for others
keep an open mind.

Before I met Carolyn, I was not interested in settling down. I had a good job, I was twenty-five, I was single, and I had a hot car. I was having a wonderful bachelor existence. But when I met Carolyn, I recognized something different had happened. You have to keep your mind open. And be open to different ideas. Before I met Carolyn, I didn't think I was going to get married until I was maybe thirty.

how rebecca *met* dave

Met on the phone: September 1999. Rebecca was twenty-five and Dave was thirty.

Met in person: November 1999 in Los Angeles, California.

Married: April 2004

I was living in Chicago and working late one night. I had just run out to grab some dinner and when I got back to work I noticed I had missed a call on my cell phone. The caller was

calling from the 310 area code—which I didn't recognize—
and hadn't left a message. This was the fourth or fifth time in
a few months that someone from the 310 area code had called
and not left a message. So, I thought, "What the heck, I want
to know who is calling me."

So I called the number. A man answered, saying his company name and his name. I asked what the company was and
why they kept calling me. I was thinking it was some kind of
telemarketer. As far as Dave was concerned, however, I had

the proper way to conduct an office romance

In the seminal 1922 work *Etiquette,* Emily Post
does not deal with the issue of workplace love.
She does, however, address the topic of having
two maids:

"In very important houses where mother and
daughter go out a great deal there are usually
two maids, one for the mother and one for the
daughter. But even in moderate households, it is
seldom practical for a debutante and her mother
to share a maid—at least during the height of
the season. That a maid who has to go out night
after night for weeks and even months on end,
and sit in the dressing room at balls until four
and five and six in the morning, is then allowed
to go to bed and to sleep until luncheon is
merely humane."

From this we can infer that, were the question asked of her, Miss Post would demonstrate
her bemusement by tittering softly behind her
handkerchief. If the wife had a job before marrying, we'd imagine Miss Post then advising,
she'd be well-served to leave at once and get to
the more pressing work of attending parties until
sunrise, making sure to forget neither her coat
nor her maid in the closet.

dialed into an unpublished number for his company, so from his perspective, I was calling the wrong number. Rather than letting the company secretary get the call, he just picked it up assuming that it was a wrong number and he could get rid of the person quickly.

I asked Dave where his company was and what it was. He said it was a record label and was located in Beverly Hills. I couldn't think of anyone I knew who worked for a record label, or worked in Beverly Hills, or even anyone who lived in Los Angeles. He told me that maybe someone from his office had dialed my number mistakenly; maybe my number was similar to the number of someone one of his coworkers knew and he or she had mistakenly dialed my number a few times over the last few months.

The conversation continued like this for a while until I gave up on figuring out the connection. I started asking about what Dave did for his job, and we segued into a general conversation. I couldn't help it—he has an incredible voice! Anyway, after about twenty minutes of chatting, it dawned on me that I knew one person in Los Angeles—a guy named Charles who had been a friend of a friend of mine in Chicago.

I asked Dave if he knew Charles; Dave said that Charles was his company's accountant. The mystery was solved. Charles had been calling my cell phone to try to get in touch with my friend in Chicago because she didn't have a cell phone and he knew we hung out a lot.

With the mystery solved, it was hard to find a great reason to keep talking without making the situation seem stranger than it already was. Dave thought maybe there was something going on between me and Charles, and he admitted later that he was kind of bummed out by that idea, even though it was so weird to even be thinking about our conversation turning into anything real. During our chat I had told him about my job and the website I ran as part of it. He went to the site and saw that there was an e-mail address to submit questions and asked if I got those questions. I said I did. He said he would e-mail me sometime, and we said goodbye.

He e-mailed me a couple hours later. Admittedly, I had waited at work until nine or ten at night to see if he would. We started e-mailing every day. After about a week, our e-mails were becoming mini-novels and we were discussing things that were better discussed over the phone, so I called him at work. We talked for a few minutes and then he asked if he could call me at home. He called me that night and we had a great, long conversation. We started talking every day, for hours on end. A few months later, I visited him in Los Angeles for the weekend. By the end of that weekend, we knew we wanted to try to keep the relationship going even though it was long distance. I had fallen in love with his voice the first time we talked. Within a few months, I was pretty sure I was in love with the rest of him.

As we grew even closer over the next few months, we discussed the possibility of living in the same city. At the same time, I was feeling like I was ready for a new job and also learned I was going to need to move out of my apartment the next summer. We weighed the pros and cons of Dave's moving to Chicago or my moving to Los Angeles. For many reasons, my moving to LA was the winning decision. I moved on July 4, 2000. After another six months, I moved into his apartment. Dave proposed on July 5, 2003.

One thing that I think really helped us grow so close was the long-distance aspect to our relationship. For over a month, we talked on the phone every day. We got to know each other in a way that I don't think happens for couples who meet in person for the first time and have a more traditional dating experience. Though we were getting to know each other extremely well, being so far way from each other allowed some anonymity. It was easier to take some risks with what we told each other because there was really nothing to lose by being totally honest. It wasn't like there was some chance that if things didn't work out, we were likely to run into each other on the street.

The result was that our relationship was built on open and honest communication from the start. That has been a key to our success in getting through difficult times. We have had our fair share of challenges in the last eight years, as most couples do, but that early bond we built has gotten us through those challenges and it continues to grow.

advice for others

don't be afraid to be with someone who challenges you.

While it may make life difficult at times, this philosophy can also lead to tremendous personal growth. Dave has this advice, which I absolutely agree with: True love happens when it happens. You'll never know when it is going to happen, and you can't plan for it. If I had listened to logic or reason, I never would have pursued this relationship.

how **belle**
met **tony**

Met: November 1995 in Kenya, Africa. Belle was thirty-five and Tony was thirty-six.

Married: November 1996

We were both volunteers for Operation Smile, a group that repairs cleft palates, in Kenya. This was my sixth trip with them. I'm a nurse, and he's a plastic surgeon. I was so impressed with him—he came with so much nice stuff, and my bags were lost until just two days before we left. We had running water for an hour in the morning. It was so hot, and there was no air conditioning in the hotel. You had to either keep the sliding doors open—and then the monkeys came in—or suffocate. Suffocate or have monkeys. We had nets over the bed against the bats. There was so much malaria in the area that the Centers for Disease Control had an outpost. And I was so hungry—I was a vegetarian. I always pack nuts, but without my suitcase, I had nothing. I was re-washing my underwear and borrowing T-shirts from people. I bought a T-shirt; on the front was the front of an elephant, on the back was the back of an elephant. There was nothing dreamy about when we first met: I was not looking cute.

I did pre- and postop. The organization recruits really great surgeons on these trips. I saw these kids come in and then saw them come out, and I was thinking, "Damn, this guy is good. I'm going to keep his card—I'm sure he can do my lips someday." I also liked his penlight. I thought he was very sharp.

What I didn't know was that maybe six or nine months before, he had lost his wife. I had heard them talking about it on an Operation Smile trip and it was terrible. We all had heard because the attending surgeon had been on many trips. He was instrumental in getting Tony to go on this trip. Tony was lined up for a meeting in Canada and said "Thanks but no thanks." But then he thought, "How often do you get invited to go to Kenya?" Nobody knew he was that guy.

It was so difficult. We worked twelve to fourteen hours a day. I was so hungry. I'd go to dinner and see some animal hanging by its ankles. Tony and I had brief encounters, but I never really talked to him. I heard him talk about his wife, so I thought he was married. The day before we left, my bags came and I was so happy. I had a Polaroid and bubbles for the kids, so I brought them to the hospital.

Everyone was running around and saying goodbye. When I saw Tony, I said, "I found this wing that has all these kids in it. Let's go and give out my stuff!" and he said, "Sure." He and I went up and down the hall and I said, "You blow the bubbles and I'll take the picture." Many of the children in the hospital were terminally ill with cancer or HIV. Some of the kids died within the hour after we left. At the same time, it was so much fun—kids love to have pictures of themselves. At one point Tony had to walk away. I didn't realize the impact it was having on him.

The last day, I hit the town square to do some shopping before our plane took off. I was a little late and I got on the plane—this small, packed, gross plane—with all the bags I'd just bought. There was one seat, next to him, and I could see his face. My arms were so full of stuff and he was thinking, "Oh great, she's sitting next to me." I plopped down and said, "These bags are so great! Did you get any for your wife?" His answer was curt: "No." Still bubbling, I said, "I got like twelve of them!" Again, his reply was brief: "I can see."

I said, "You can have as many as you want." He answered, "I don't have a wife to get a bag for." When I told him that I thought he was married, he said, "Oh, no, my wife recently died."

I remembered the story and I was shocked. I just started bawling. Tears were just falling down my face. He told me he was so happily married that he didn't want to be single and all these women were coming out of the woodwork. He said, "I'd like companionship, but I don't want to go on a date—if I call them back, they think we're getting married. It's so stressful I just don't answer my phone."

And then he said, "What about you? What did you get for your boyfriend?" I said, "I don't do boys anymore." I had been in love with this guy, I loved everything about him—I loved his tennis shoes. But he didn't love me, and it was just so hard to get over that. We were good friends, a perfect fit, had all these things in common, but he didn't agree. I had always wanted to be a mom, and I would think, "Why can't I get this together?"

Then I started wondering, "Why can't I be a mom on my own? I have good things to pass on." So I started the proceedings for adoptions. You have to get friends to say you're normal and you have to get fingerprinted. I told Tony all this and that this was my last trip on Operation Smile; I knew I wouldn't be able to take off and go to some foreign country. I told him, "I'm suffering from a broken heart and decided to move on and I'm adopting a baby."

This conversation all happened within an hour. We landed in Nairobi and went our separate ways. I went on to California and he to Colorado. I didn't want to say, "Call me some day." When I got home, there was a message from him saying, "I just want to see if you got home okay." I called him. We developed a friendship—just a friendship. We'd call and send faxes. He wanted to come visit me and he said, "I don't want to lead you on," and I said, "That's okay."

the white wedding

According to the *Encyclopedia of Clothes and Fashion,* the white wedding dress was introduced in 1816 by Queen Victoria's cousin, Crown Princess Charlotte. "According to reports . . . her bridal gown consisted of a silver tissue and lace overgown worn over a white underdress." She wasn't trying to make any virginal statement; her gown "probably had more to do with the Regency fashion of white dresses than any symbolic intent." The white "ideal" came a few decades later, in 1840, "when Queen Victoria wore a creamy white Spitalfields silk satin and lace gown." That's the mama of the dresses we think of when we think "wedding dress": "It was endlessly reproduced in fashion journals, setting a fashion standard for some appreciable time."

That's how we started. I went to visit him, and we just fell in love with each other. It was just perfect. It just happened. No way you could have orchestrated it differently. We went on different trips together—we went to Israel, the West Bank. The next fall we were going to go to China. He proposed to me beforehand, and we eloped. He came out one weekend and we eloped and we went to China the next day.

I got back to California after visiting Tony the first time, and the adoption social worker said to me, "I smell something different about you. Are you by any chance in love?" And I said, "Well, I think I could be." She said, "You need to put this on hold and we can always open your file again. You need to make sure this is something you really want to do." Later, it turned out that she was right; I didn't want to follow through with the adoption. We tried for a family but it never happened. We just take care of each other.

advice for others

there's something to be said for faith and knowing yourself.

You can try on your own to pick a husband that fits. Sometimes you hit it and sometimes you don't. But if you believe in God and ask sincerely, I believe he'll pick the best one for you. It also doesn't hurt to be a little older and have some maturity under your belt.

how julie
met jeff

Met: May 2000 in Pittsburgh, Pennsylvania. Julie was twenty-two and Jeff was twenty-seven.

Married: March 2001

I met the love of my life at a psychiatric hospital.

After graduating from college, I decided to take a year off and work before going to graduate school. I accepted a position as direct care staff at a psychiatric hospital in Pittsburgh. It was a difficult place to work. Most of the staff members were jerks. It was pretty intense at times—it was in-patient psych work, so the patients were pretty severe. Most were adolescents who had tried to kill themselves or had threatened or tried to harm others. At times, we had to restrain kids to help them calm down and not harm themselves or others. It was a hard job.

From early on, I kept noticing this cute guy. I came to find out that his name was Jeff and that he worked in the admissions department. The first time I talked to him, we were both in the nurses' station on one of the hospital units. We talked a few times. Each time I saw him I got butterflies in my stomach—he was just so cute and seemed so sweet. But I never thought he was interested in me, and our conversations were usually just in passing.

One St. Patrick's Day, a Saturday, I was working a long shift, from three in the morning until three in the afternoon. By the time the 7 A.M. staff came in, I looked horrible and was exhausted. Meanwhile, Jeff had volunteered to work on the wards that weekend to make a little extra money. He showed up at 7 A.M., and we ended up working together for a whole shift. We talked the entire time.

At some point toward the end of the shift, he asked me what I was doing that night. I said that I had no plans and he arranged to pick me up later, after he was done working. I came home that day, before we even went on our first date, and told my mom that I had met the guy I was going to marry. She said something like, "He sounds like a really great guy," but that was about it. I had just ended a really bad relationship and she hated my ex-boyfriend, so I think she was a little leery. But I just somehow knew that Jeff was the one— the feeling hit me really strong, and to feel so intensely about someone so soon after the breakup was really surprising to me. But the chemistry was amazing.

It was St. Patrick's Day so we figured we should go out to a bar. The funny thing is that neither of us is really a bar kind of person. But we didn't realize that until later. So Jeff picked me up and we went to Margaritaville, a bar on the south side of Pittsburgh. The whole time we stood and sat really close and talked. It was like we were the only two people in the bar. Our first kiss was later that night when he dropped me off at home.

It felt like we had known each other forever and had so much to talk about. I can't explain it completely in words, but it just felt like a great fit. Three and a half years later, he proposed, I said yes, and, just as I predicted, on St. Patrick's Day 2001, I ended up marrying him. He's my best friend and soul mate—pretty good for a match made in a psychiatric hospital!

advice for others
things happen for a reason.

I had only ended my bad relationship a few weeks before Jeff asked me out on our first date. When I broke up with my ex, I was convinced that I would never meet a good guy. Then, all of the sudden, this guy who I had thought was cute for months comes along and it was instantaneous. It was like someone had a plan that things would work out that way for us. Jeff told me later that he had basically given up on meeting the right person before he met me and was becoming more accepting of the fact that maybe he would just be single. We found each other when we both were least expecting it but needed it the most.

friends first

*I*n 2000, researchers from the University of Washington announced they had developed a one-hour interview that could predict newlyweds' marital stability in the years to come with 87 percent accuracy. The interview, they said, measures a couple's all-important "marital bond."

"Part of the marital bond is the global or perceptual filter couples have of the relationship," says study co-author Kim Buehlman. "If you have a strong marital bond, you give your partner a break when times are tough. With a strong bond, even if a couple doesn't agree on something, they find ways of avoiding destructive arguments because they really like each other and appreciate the differences. With a weak bond, you don't give respect and kindness to your partner. There is a lot more disagreement and a lot less friendship."

All the people I interviewed for this book mentioned how lucky they are to have their spouse for a friend. The couples in this chapter are possibly even luckier. For them, friendship came first.

how rebecca *met* greg

Met: September 1990 in Jerusalem, Israel. Rebecca and Greg were both twenty.

Married: June 1996

We were both studying abroad in our junior year of college. The first time I met Greg, he was dating my friend Sharon. When she introduced us, no lightning struck, but we became friends. When we went back to our colleges in Washington, D.C., we kept hanging out. We introduced our roommates, who then dated, and the four of us went out often. I found Greg very easy to talk to. Our relationship was a combination of deep conversations, Jewish activism, and bar hopping. It's funny because I actually did date a lot of my friends over the years, but I was just always very satisfied with my friendship with Greg. I dated other people and he was with someone else the whole time.

I wasn't longing for Greg. Though we like to tease each other, "You were pining away for me," I don't think either one of was. During my senior year, we had a formal for my sorority. I remember holding out for a real date. I didn't find one, so finally Greg invited himself. I said, "Well if I can't find someone else, I guess I'll have to settle for a friend."

I don't remember how things changed, I really don't. Eventually, after we were out of school and we were both single, we both just started thinking about it. We went to New York for a New Year's party and he was very flirty—rubbing my back, holding my hand. The next weekend, my roommate and our two friends across the hall were planning a big party. We were calling it "The Party of the Century." He invited me over during the week for dinner, but I couldn't go; I had to shop for the party.

At that point I knew something was going to happen with us. I remember looking across the room at him at the party and thinking, "I'm going to kiss him." Late in the evening, after most of the people had gone, we went outside. I had a recurring problem with my front door key not working the first few times I tried it, and as I was working it, he kissed me. He always says I didn't open the door on purpose, but the key really didn't work. I was leaving for Israel a month later to study for six months. You know how at the end of summer camp you hook up with someone? It took away some of the pressure of, "What does this mean?"

We kept in touch—we wrote letters, talked, and he came to visit me at home in New Jersey before I left. A lot of our relationship developed through our writing, and then he came to visit me in Israel.

I think part of our getting together when we did was that I wasn't finding anyone else that interesting. I dated a lot of people as I got older. And I guess part of it was that as you get older, friendships become more significant. But then after the first kiss, it wasn't clear where it was going. For me, I was kind of going with it while he was saying, "It's going to mess up our friendship." The whole fact I was leaving town took the stress off it for me; you don't have to define it when you're going away.

But it became something, obviously. Reflecting back, I think sometimes it was easier because it wasn't the same kind of games with a friend. It's not perfect; marriage isn't.

But because we had that basis in friendship and the ability to communicate and listen to what the other person needs, we've stayed strong. And the thing is that even if things aren't perfect, I really can't imagine a better fit.

advice to others

do your thing (just do something).

I never was the meet-someone-at-a-bar type of person. I met guys through mutual friends and common interests. And I liked to spend time as friends first. Part of it is I'm shy and that's a way of getting more comfortable and the emotional aspect of it was important to me. Do your thing, and try to meet people with common interests. Pursue your own activities; participate in what you are interested in. And then again, a relationship may come from nowhere that you expect.

how susan *met* ned

Met: September 1981 in Philadelphia, Pennsylvania. Both Sue and Ned were eighteen.

Married: July 1984

We were in the Van Pelt House dorm at Penn sophomore year. I guess we met at a party that night. I really don't remember meeting Ned, but he remembers meeting me. I think it was the first night of school and everyone was moving in. The professor in charge of the dorm gave a party. The next day, Ned asked me if I wanted to go get some milk with him at the twenty-four-hour market. I said no.

Later on, I ran into him in between classes and he teased me that I had missed out on a great time. That's when I suddenly noticed him. He had this long blond ponytail and blue eyes—he looked like a preppy rebel—and suddenly I thought he was cute and that light switched on. And then we were together a lot.

We had meals every night together with our friends in the 200-person dining hall. Ned was just a few dorm rooms down the hall. We were just friends. It didn't evolve for a while. He had never had a girlfriend, but I had had lots of boyfriends, so I assumed that eventually we were just going to start dating each other.

Maybe a month into getting to know him, I was trimming his beard and I suggested that we date and he said something like, "I don't think I'm ready for that." I was insulted but I kept my cool. I started seeing other people and stayed friends with him. We had this low-key sexual tension for almost the whole year. I found him very interesting and funny. He introduced me to Kurt Vonnegut and to mellow music. We ate cereal in his room late at night. One night, we were talking about our favorite books as kids. He told me his was *James and the Giant Peach* and he said my face reminded him of a peach. He reached over and stroked my face. It was one of the most romantic nights of my life.

Spring of that year he went home to New York and cut his ponytail off. He came back and looked really great. Some girl said, "Ned's haircut has made him the most eligible man in

quote/
unquote

> "It is not a lack of love, but a lack of friendship that makes unhappy marriages."
> —Friedrich Nietzsche

Van Pelt House." All I could think was, "I got there first!" and then I realized, even if we're always friends, it's fine because I love our friendship. That same night, he kissed me and everything changed. I don't know what changed in his mind. I think his new haircut turned him into a new person.

That night we were studying on my bed, like we had always done. He had his head in my lap. We were that comfortable with each other but I still never dared to believe it would ever become something else. But I wanted it to, like crazy. In fact, another guy once asked me out to the movies and I brought Ned along—we used to go to every movie together. When the guy asked me to another movie, he said, "Can we go without Ned?" and I said no.

But that night Ned and I kissed. He says he kissed me first. I don't remember it that way, but I have stopped arguing about it—it's been twenty-five years.

advice for others

have fun.

I think that you really have to be able to have fun, the way you have fun with a really, really good friend. After you've been together this long, there's often not nearly the same sort of rush you associate with love, so you have to have a whole relationship to fall back on. Together you can come up with ways to keep that alive. Ned really is my best friend, and that friendship does not get in the way of sexual excitement. It's all part of our relationship. We can talk about anything. I guess others might need mystery, but I need to be able to talk about anything with him. It has to be a full relationship and not just a spark.

how lindsey met john

Met: January 1997 in College Station, Texas. Lindsey was nineteen and John was eighteen.

Married: February 2008

I was a sophomore in college just back from my winter break. At the time I lived with three girlfriends, and we were getting ready to go out. One of them had a friend over who had brought along with him his best friend and a fraternity pledge, John. John was there for maybe an hour. But I was actually interested in the other guy and ended up dating him for three years.

John and I were just really good friends all through college. I went with him to pick out lingerie for his girlfriend when she was in town. While I was living in Los Angeles, he moved to the Washington, D.C., area. I had always wanted to go to D.C.; I had never been that far east. But I moved back to Texas in March 2003.

John and I planned for me to come out and visit—just friends getting together to hang out. It was normal the first night. We went out and partied, still in the platonic phase. We came home and went to sleep.

The next night, we went out and something changed. We started to flirt with each other and be cheesy and lame and hold hands. We ended up hooking up that night, Friday. But I don't think I started realizing, "Aw, I kinda like him" until I was getting on the plane to leave. I could feel the mood shifting while I was with him, but it was more along the lines of "He's hot, I'm having fun. I'm enjoying the weekend, why not, we're both single, who cares?" And then Sunday, I was really bummed when it came to be time to leave. Getting on the airplane, I realized that I was thinking, "I like John. Oh man!"

I think it probably took him longer. When I left, he admitted later, he felt really sad that I was leaving, but I don't think he realized why he was sad. He called me three or four times a week. When I went to visit him again in July, we finally both realized we did like each other. We kept it casual because it was long distance, but we talked almost every night and sent lots of instant messages and text messages. I came out whenever I could and he came whenever he could, and then in December he broke up with me.

He decided neither of us was ready to move for the other one and he didn't want a long-distance relationship anymore. He said, "I want to find someone in town who I can see all the time." I was heartbroken.

marriage in biblical times

It is written in Deuteronomy that if a man dies without children, his brother must marry the deceased man's wife and name their first child for the dead man. And if he refuses, she can take his sandal and spit on him.

Three months later he started calling again. I said, "What do you want? Leave me alone." He said, "I made a mistake. I want to be together, really together. I want you to move here." I was scared because I wanted to just date. We dated four or five months, and then in the fall I said, "Okay, let's try it." I had some stuff to finish up so I stayed in Texas until March 2005. John came out and helped me pack the U-Haul.

There's no formal romantic engagement story. John is pretty traditional; he grew up in a very Catholic family. I was always "eh" about marriage. I'm not totally opposed to it. I just didn't understand why people felt they had to marry. I was happy with the way things were. But when I went to my sister's wedding I thought, "Oh, I understand now. My sister is in love, and she wants to share it with family and friends."

John and I started talking more about us. When my grandmother died, my dad gave me the inheritance money and said I should do something special with it. I thought, "A ring is something special I can keep forever—instead of blowing it on clothes." So John and I split the cost of the ring (he insisted on contributing), and I donated the rest of the inheritance money to the hospice that had cared for my grandmother.

A month later, we had the perfect, most romantic wedding, before thirty guests.

advice for others
be friends first.

I think our relationship is really strong because it has such a strong foundation of being friends for so long. We weren't best friends, but I feel we have a deeper bond than friends our age in relationships. We have a great respect for each other, and we enjoy spending so much time together because we are such solid friends.

chapter 9

the blind date

ou can't have reached a certain age without collecting some great blind date stories. My personal favorite (so far) is the guy who asked me, just after the terrorist attacks of September 11, 2001, if I was afraid to fly. I said that I was. I had actually flown from California to Washington, D.C., at the end of August and had been nervous enough about a security guard's talking to her friend instead of watching the screen as the luggage rolled through the X-ray machine that I flagged down her supervisor to complain. I didn't have any plans to fly right away, I told him, but if I had been holding tickets for a trip I'd already planned, I still would have gotten on the plane. I thought we were talking about going forward after that great tragedy, but it turns out we weren't.

"Are you afraid in general?" he asked.

"Um, no," I said.

"Because you can buy a gun if you are."

"For the plane?" I asked, probably agog.

"No, for your house. You can have a gun for your house."

"I think," I said carefully, trying to continue, "that if someone wanted to take a gun from me and use it himself, he probably wouldn't have a problem."

"You could keep it in your purse," he offered helpfully. "A little one."

"Are you telling me to conceal a weapon?"

"You can have a little gun in your purse if you're afraid," he repeated. And I'm pretty sure he made a motion of putting something—like a gun—in a bag and snapping it shut.

The date did not improve. I even took a phone call from a friend I was due to meet in a few hours and, when she told me she would be late, said, "Oh great, I'll be there in twenty minutes." (I swear I have pulled this move only once.)

But sometimes the announcement "I know just the guy for you" doesn't precede a painful evening. One guy I know really knocked nervously on his blind date's door in the early evening and then, after escorting her home late at night, called his dad to say, "I've met the girl I'm going to marry."

He's not the only one. These are the stories couples have of how a simple cup of coffee led to the first day of the rest of their lives—together.

how kayla *met* keith

Met on the phone: November 2005

Met in person: December 2005 in Houston, Texas. Kayla was twenty-six and Keith was twenty-seven.

Married: November 2007

The night I found out I had failed the Texas bar exam also happened to be my birthday, so I went out to a bar with a friend who had just passed it. My friend called her "big brother"

Keith—actually a friend of hers from law school in New York City. I had taken a big break from dating and felt like I was ready to get out there again, so I was getting out there. And I had let my friends know that.

When my friend called Keith, she handed me the phone. I talked to him for a bit, making small talk and thinking nothing of it. When she took the phone back, he told her I sounded cute. She realized I only dated guys who were bad for me and didn't care about me, and she said, "He is probably the closest I know to being good enough for you."

Then she started in on us having to meet each other.

A month or so passed, and we talked to each other again on the phone. We would also send book-length e-mails every day. I really thought I would never meet him in person, so I could totally be myself. He was intelligent and funny. We asked each other a lot of questions and shared a lot of insights. We had a lot to talk about, and I felt like I had a pretty good idea of who he was. I knew he was honest, ambitious, interesting, and a hard worker. I don't know how much of that was biased by my friend's input, though. She spoke so highly of him, and she is one of my closest friends, so I guess her opinion counted for a lot.

My friend had a New Year's Day party, and Keith came out from Denver to meet me in person. I felt like I knew him from talking to him on the phone but I have never been good at blind dates. Plus, he was here to just meet me and that freaked me out a bit. It was awkward. I was also dating some other people when I met him. I was so nervous. He had a dozen white roses for me, a bag of Reese's Pieces, my favorite candy, and a pet rock from a personal joke we had on the phone. It was romantic, and I felt special.

Eventually, I became less nervous. We went to dinner and the aquarium and we rode the Ferris wheel.

It was just so easy being with Keith. It was easy to talk to him, like I was talking to someone who "got" me. I wasn't used to that. Right before he left, he wanted me to know he did not intend to date anyone else. And I said, "Uh . . . not yet." I wanted my freedom—and I was scared.

After that weekend, we didn't see each other. I was taking the bar exam again, and he knew that was my priority, but we talked nearly every night. We talked—sometimes for hours—about different topics ranging from what we had for dinner to religion and politics and family and then our hopes and dreams. We didn't agree on everything—for example, I am conservative and he is liberal, but we could see each other's point. It was like dating, but we didn't get to see each other. I liken it to dating in Orthodox Judaism: talking but no touching.

A few weeks later, I was at lunch with some friends and someone asked, "How would you feel if he was talking to someone else?" I realized that I didn't like the thought of it at all. When I got home, I called him and just blurted out, "I want to be your girlfriend," because I am oh so smooth like that. And after a couple months of traveling back and forth, it just felt right, so we both started looking for jobs in each other's cities. He found one first and moved here to Houston in July.

advice for others
know what you need.

When I was younger, I wanted someone who wanted to have fun and didn't care what I did and was very different from my parents and my family. I learned that I was wrong. You need to have responsibility. What I thought was wrong with my family was really what I wanted—security and stability and love and support and really looking into someone's heart to find who they are. I guess I just grew up.

---

how **sarah** *met* **ted**

Met: June 2006, in Columbia, Maryland. Sarah was thirty-three and Ted was thirty-five.

Married: May 2008

It was a completely blind date; we had been set up by mutual friends. I was in my mid-thirties and had been on many dates, both blind and otherwise, and also in a couple of long-term relationships. I had heard people talk about meeting "the One," and to be honest, I thought it was complete garbage. I am a scientist by training, so I have a completely analytical mind. I am very literal, reasonable, and methodical in my daily life and work. The idea that I could suddenly meet someone and know that he was the one seemed plastic and unreal. Experiences like that were for more romantic-minded people—musicians, artists, and actors. I have always liked the idea of being sensible. I figured I would leave the wildly romantic stories for soap operas, movies, and television.

But when Ted said "Good evening" and I sat down and started talking with him, I remember thinking, "Every other guy, every other boyfriend, every other fling has just been practice." This guy was it. Even in my analytical, reasonable, logical, and methodical mind, I knew it. I didn't know if he felt the same way, but there was absolutely no question in my mind. If Ted agreed that we would pursue a relationship, then I would fight harder for it than anything else in my life.

I still have no concrete idea what it was about that first meeting, but the thing that really struck me was the simple way he looked straight at me and didn't let his eyes wander around the room. I knew that he was actually listening and responding, rather than thinking of the next thing to say. Then there were the eyes themselves—blue, warm, and friendly, but with

quote unquote

"At some point in life, most of us will face a major mental-health crisis. It is called love . . . Studies in Italy looking at blood levels of the brain chemical serotonin have suggested that love and mental illness have much in common. They compared serotonin levels of people recently in love; patients with obsessive-compulsive disorder; and a 'control' group that was neither. The researchers found that the love-struck participants showed a drop in serotonin levels similar to those with obsessive-compulsive problems."

—*Wall Street Journal*

this mischievous glint that made me grateful I hadn't gotten stuck baby-sitting him years earlier!

Maybe it was the multiple things we had in common—family, athletics, a love of children—or our shared desires for our future. Maybe it was part physical attraction, or maybe it was just two people meeting each other at the exact right time in their lives. Whatever it was, it stuck. Sure, there have been a few small bumps along the road, but 99 percent of the time, our relationship is easier than anything else I have experienced in my life. I wish I had a more scientific way to explain it, but it just feels absolutely right.

Despite our common interests, I also now realize that the list of things we disagree on is nearly as long as the list of things we agree on. I have looked at him and wondered how it could be that we're so different and yet love each other so very much. Every other relationship I've had just stopped when I thought about going forward as a serious couple. With Ted, I see our clear path forward. I want him with me.

advice for others
be picky and be you.

Looking back on my previous relationship, which really wasn't all that bad but also wasn't all that great, I shudder to think of where I would be now if I hadn't woken up to go after what I really wanted. Ted was nowhere near when I called off my previous relationship. I just knew that my ex was not the one for me. I couldn't see him as someone I would spend the rest of my life with. So I gave myself the luxury of being picky and a few months later, Ted came into my life.

I think it's easy to get caught up with what we all envision as the perfect life: children, a job, marriage. I think it is also imperative that a person really evaluates what she wants out of life. Even if it doesn't match exactly what society tells us you should want, go after what you want. Screw everyone else—they can live their own lives.

The one thing that continues to convince me that Ted is the guy for me is that I don't have to change a single thing about myself for the relationship to work. I don't walk on eggshells, I don't sit on my opinions, and I don't have to change how I look, talk, or communicate.

how amy *met* dale

Met: April 1998 in Charleston, South Carolina. Amy was twenty-seven and Dale was twenty-eight.
Married: May 1999

I met Dale on a blind date set up by my mom and her golf teacher, Rocky. She and my stepdad Charlie are both golfers and members at a private club; Rocky was getting married and invited them to his wedding. He said one of his groomsmen had just moved to Atlanta from Charleston and didn't have a date. Rocky and my mom thought, "We'll set them up."

They thought we would get along because we're both laid back. Dale tells me now he agreed because my parents and my sister were going to the wedding, so in his mind it wouldn't be a disaster if we didn't hit it off because I would have other people to talk to. I was twenty-seven at the time and thinking, "I might not meet the right person and I just have to live with that. I'll be an old maid."

The wedding was Saturday, and Dale came in on Thursday night. I went with my sister and her boyfriend to a bar downtown that night, the Blind Tiger. I remember looking at the guys coming in and thinking, "I hope that's not him" and "I hope that's not him." But when Dale walked in, I felt this instant connection and I thought, "That's it. Okay, this is the guy." It might seem crazy, but I really believed it. We hung out that night for a couple of hours just talking. I remember it was a little awkward—he was quiet, so I had to do a lot of the talking. I was thinking, "Ooh, he's not so chatty. We'll have to see."

The next night was the rehearsal dinner—the blind date was over a whole weekend. He was doing all kinds of wedding stuff. The dinner was a half-hour drive away, and I was supposed to be following my sister and her boyfriend out there. She's younger but she didn't want to deal with me tagging along, and I remember feeling awkward having to drive myself there. I made myself go. When I walked in, he was standing in the corner talking to my parents. I thought, "This is another good sign." I walked up to him and the conversation was easier that night. He walked me to the car and we had our first kiss.

The next day was the wedding. I was going to the reception but not the ceremony. I thought he was going to call when he was on the way to the reception. I was all dressed up, but he never called. I was so surprised. I thought we had a connection.

I talked to my sister, who was also just going to the reception and she said, "Just go." I said, "When you see him there, tell him he was supposed to call me." My mom later said when they got there he came up and said, "Where's Amy?" And he was stunned when she said, "She's at home waiting for you to call." He thought I was just supposed to come.

I was home giving myself a pep talk, thinking, "This is too big a deal. Swallow your pride. You've got to just suck it up and go." So I drove to the reception by myself and had to walk in by myself and go and find him. It was a little awkward. But I saw him and we immediately had a great time together. We danced, and he came home and spent the night, and the next morning he drove back to Atlanta. We exchanged phone calls, and I e-mailed him a couple of days later to suggest that he come back the next weekend. It was the first time I really pushed myself with a guy. He e-mailed right back and said he would.

When it came to whether Dale was the man I wanted to marry, it wasn't even a question. I just knew. But I had a lot of doubts about marriage in general. I always knew I wanted to get married, but coming from a divorced family, I was never sure that marriage would work for me. I'm still not sure. I hope so, but I've seen what happens, and I had a hard time when we were planning our wedding. I always wondered, "What will make us work when my parent's marriage didn't work?"

do you take this cheese?

"The highlight of the Grape Festival held each year in Nauvoo, Illinois, is the historical pageant known as the Wedding of the Wine and Cheese . . . In the pageant there is a marriage ceremony celebrating the union of cheese and wine in which a magistrate reads the marriage contract, places it between the wine (carried by the bride) and the cheese (carried by the groom), and circles all three with a wooden hoop symbolizing the wedding ring."

—*Holidays, Festivals, and Celebrations of the World Dictionary*

I think when we were dating, I learned to trust Dale, and because I trusted him, I didn't worry as much about everything else. (Until we started actually planning and then reality kicked in!) I think a big part of learning to trust him came out of how well he handled my diabetes. He wasn't scared away from the ups and downs of my disease, like other boyfriends had been. Instead, he was really a rock when it came to all that. So for the first time in my life, I could let someone see the real me.

advice for others
keep busy.

I would hate to say "Be patient" because it's the last thing you want to hear. The majority of people I knew married their college boyfriends right after graduation. I had gotten to the point that I thought I might not meet anybody, and I was depressed about that. So I went out and filled up my free time with all kinds of stuff, like running a marathon and volunteering. Dale was so impressed with everything I was involved in. We laugh about it now. I filled my life up with extracurricular activities so I wasn't sitting at home feeling sorry for myself. And of course they all fell to the wayside when we met.

how amy met mike

Met: June 1997 in Cincinnati, Ohio. Amy was twenty-six and Mike was twenty-seven.

Married: October 1998

I was living in Cincinnati. I had gone to school there and decided to stay after graduation. My good friend Anna told me about her ex-boyfriend Mike from Ohio who had called her out of the blue. Anna and Mike had dated in high school, and they kept in touch on and off through their early adult years. She had gotten married, had a kid, and then gotten divorced. He knew that. He had recently gotten out of a three-year relationship and called her to say, "Hey, we never resolved that." He set up a time to come to Cincinnati to see her.

Anna told me, "This ex-boyfriend is coming to visit me and I haven't told him everything that's going on in my life." The reason she had gotten divorced was she had figured out she was a lesbian. She didn't exactly know how to tell Mike over the phone.

When Mike came, he saw the family picture up on her wall and met Anna's partner, Cindy. They talked about it, and he understood. Anna called him later in the week and said, "I have a good friend I work with and I'd really like you to meet her." When she told me about Mike, I was happily living my life, but for some reason I decided to go ahead and give him my number. He called, and we talked once or twice and set up a date. He would come to Cincinnati for a Reds game—I knew he was a sports fan.

One thing frightened me. Anna had said, "He's bulky and he has three tattoos." And I said, "Tattoos?" I was of the opinion anyone with tattoos was a complete freak. I thought, "Oh my God, I am going to go out with this tattoo man." The other thing she had told me was he was from Cleveland, the west side. I was from the east side.

When Mike was in high school, his father transferred to Indiana. That's where he met Anna. She said he liked the Indians and the Browns—both teams I like. Seemed we might have some things in common. So I decided we'd go to a Reds game. But on the day of our date it was pouring rain, and they called off the Reds game. Mike parked in the driveway and knocked on the door. I thought, "What am I going to do now? I don't really have a whole big backup plan." I was afraid, I didn't know what to expect. I trusted Anna but, again, I was a little standoffish about the tattoos.

We had lunch at Wendy's. It was close and simple. I got a salad, which I proceeded to spill all over myself. The next meal—in fact, our first three meals together—I had salads and spilled them all over myself. I always spill my food. We went down to Union Terminal and went to the history museum. We had a great time. From there, we talked on the phone a couple more times and saw each other a couple weeks later.

It got pretty serious pretty quickly. Mike moved down to Cincinnati by the end of August. My best friend from high school had gone away for the summer with her husband and when she came back she said to me, "Oh my God. You met this guy, he's moved in with you. This is so not you!"

It only took me a month to realize that I was in love. I had visited Mike in Colorado and met his family. We talked about his moving to Cleveland. Little did he know he'd find a job very quickly. We had talked about him getting an apartment. But at that point we figured we should be together even though we hadn't lived in the same city yet. It didn't make sense to pay two rents and two utility bills. I said, "Why don't you live with me and if it doesn't work, you can move somewhere else."

We combined all of our money right away. He showed me all his bills, threw it all on the table and we dealt with it from there. We put all of our stuff into the computer and made the expenses and finances go together right away. There was no hesitation. I think that's when I knew he was in this for good. He was baring everything.

But the job he found wasn't a great one and by December he had found another in Colorado. At that point we had already decided we were going to get married. I quit my job, moved out to Colorado, and we got married on Halloween. We had a ceremony in the church but the reception was a costume party. I didn't let him dress up. He's a groom one day in his life and that's what he's going to be.

advice for others
bare your soul.

Be willing to be open, to adapt, and to bring somebody else in. Communicate. Not to sound corny, but bare your soul so you know where you each stand. Before we moved in, we were writing letters and talking every day. We talked about what our feelings were, our goals and aspirations. I believe it was Anna who gave me *The Book of Questions*. We went through it question by question and page by page and let each person answer. That really helped us learn about each other.

His parents had gotten divorced after twenty years of marriage, and my parents were divorced. We were kind of skeptical: Would we work? I think that was common ground for us. We watched a whole boatload of broken marriages. We saw not-right relationships. We wanted to make sure this was the right thing for both of us before we fully committed, but at the same time I think we fully committed very early on.

how kimberly *met* thomas

Met: November 2003 in Walla Walla, Oregon. Kimberly was twenty-five and Thomas was twenty-eight.

Married: July 2006

I was living in Portland. Lindsay, my very good friend in Walla Walla, called me and asked if I would accompany one of her friends to a work event because he didn't have a date.

He didn't want to ask a local Walla Wallan because it's a small town and people talk. She never said the word "date." She said, "It's only one night and we can just hang the rest of the weekend." I visited Lindsay every couple of months. So even though I was seeing someone at the time (I was nearing the end of a relatively long, dramatic, bad relationship), I agreed, thinking it would be a harmless night out.

Thomas and I met the night before the event. I had just driven into town and was at Lindsay's. Thomas had worked late and came over. I remember when Thomas walked in he made a beeline for the kitchen. He showed me an Edward Gory book, showed me the details, what he liked about it and why he thought it was so cool. It was sweet.

I thought he was incredible looking. He's a very striking looking person with shoulder-length curly hair. Gorgeous. But I was in a relationship, and he knew it. I thought he was really attractive but wasn't looking at him as a reason for me to break up with my boyfriend.

Well, the night out turned out to be an auction. Because the winery Thomas worked for had donated some items, he was chosen to go. The auction and dinner were predictably dull, as most people there were more interested in the wine lots than the cause. But Thomas was kind and continually attentive and funny. We ditched the auction early and met up with our friends at a local bar before deciding to go dancing at the only place in town. Thomas and I spent the rest of the night dancing and sitting in a corner on the couch talking and talking.

will you be my happily ever after?

Which of the famous writers below met his or her spouse on a blind date?

A. Amy Tan
B. Judy Blume
C. J. K. Rowling
D. Stephen King

Answer: A, B, and C.

A. Amy Tan met her attorney husband Lou DeMattei on a blind date while making her sixth attempt at college. Her mom didn't speak to her for six months when she chose to follow DeMattei from Oregon to California—but Tan did finally earn her bachelor's degree (and go on for her master's) once she got to San Jose.

B. Judy Blume's setup was blessed by her future stepdaughter. As Blume told the *Washington Post,* she had been divorced from her first husband and was living in New Mexico when George Cooper, also divorced, came to town to visit his twelve-year-old daughter, Amanda. "A friend gave him a list of five women who could be potential dinner partners during his stay," she told the reporter. "He showed the list to Amanda and asked for her input. She took one look at the name 'Judy Blume' and started shrieking."

C. *Harry Potter* author, J.K. Rowling met her husband, Dr. Neil Murray, in Scotland in 2000, thanks to a setup by a mutual friend.

D. Stephen King met his wife Tabitha when both were in school at the University of Maine.

We don't remember what we talked about. It wasn't anything important or especially interesting. Whatever you talk about when it's three in the morning and you've had a lot to drink. We just remember that it felt really good and not acknowledging anything that was going on between us. Soon it was five in the morning. He had to drive to Seattle at seven to catch a flight, so he dropped Lindsay and me at her house before going home to pack for his trip.

As we said goodbye at the door, he gave me an amazing hug but quickly left. If we had kissed it would have spoiled everything. It would have crossed the line—because I was in a relationship. It was so perfect just hanging in that moment. You know when you're a little kid and you think what it's going to be like when all the pieces fit? I could have just bottled it up and taken it down and smelled it. As he was leaving town, he stopped by the house and left me a business card from a Thai restaurant with a note saying what an amazing time he had. I still have it.

I couldn't even sleep that night, I was so excited about meeting him and kept reliving it in my mind. It is still one of the most memorable and best nights I've ever had with him. After that weekend, I went home and broke up with my boyfriend.

Thomas and I began dating in early December. We kept it pretty casual because of the distance and because I was still getting over my breakup. I was holding him at arm's length and ended up breaking up with him in August. We talked on the phone four or five times after that, and I knew he was dating other girls.

I went home to Cleveland for Christmas. I was mopey. I told my mom about breaking up with Thomas, that he was dating other people and I felt so stupid. She said, "Well, just call him."

On January 3, I called him. He was driving home from Seattle for New Year's. It started as a, "Hey how are you?" but it was a good talk. We talked for a while. And then I kind of brought up the subject of getting together and seeing each other and he said he'd be in Portland in the next month or so. When we got back together, there were no games. We were in it.

advice for others
it shouldn't be hard work.

If it's meant to be, it's going to come easy. It's not going to be forced. We kept saying to each other we never felt like we worked on our relationship. We did, and we still do, but it's intuitive. We talk a lot and each of us knows where the other is, but we don't ever feel like we have to plan ahead for each other, plan ahead to talk. It just happens; we do it because we want to. We really understand how to speak to each other. We both had long relationships that weren't great. We know what not to do. We know what we like and don't like and know how not to treat someone. I'm not saying we have a perfect relationship. But we don't pull bull on each other, which makes it feel easy. Maybe as we age and go along we'll have spots where it's not so easy. In the past, though, we tried to force relationships to work. At the end of the day you're exhausted. If it's not going to work, it's not going to work, and all you've done is waste a lot of time and energy.

going out when you want to stay in

At the end of the day, I want to pick up a book. It's that simple. I want to stretch out on my couch with my dog and a book and relax. (I also like to wake up at six to walk said dog before going to the yoga studio, so events that start at ten at night appeal as much to me as getting up at six in the morning to walk a dog and practice yoga does to others.) The thing is, as I once told a friend who wanted very much to marry but, like me, is less than a social butterfly, the right girl isn't (currently) in your living room.

So we get up. We go out on New Year's Eve, even though forced merriment is one of the harder things in life to swallow. We go to a bar when the band is playing bluegrass, like Jill did. We even go out when life is at its hardest, as John and Daisy did. They each got up off the couch after they had suffered the loss of a spouse. And because they did, they found each other.

I'll never forget the friend, now long married, who had to be guilted into going to a Halloween party. She was tired; she didn't think it would be any fun to be surrounded by people dressed as witches and pirates. But she found her husband there. As she told me, eyes wide, still amazed by her near miss, "I didn't want to go that night."

how john *met* serena

Met: New Year's Eve 2003 in Washington, D.C. John was twenty-nine and Serena was thirty-three.

Married: March 2005

My friend Kathryn from grad school and several of her friends and acquaintances organized a party at Saint Ex, a bar in D.C. It was one of those deals where they rent out the bar, and each guest pays $75 to get in. Then the food and, more importantly, the drinks were "free." I decided to come to D.C. and have a more rockin' New Year than I would have had home visiting my parents in North Carolina.

I met up with Susanne, a woman I dated for a while in grad school. She had met Kathryn while in D.C. and knew a few of my other friends. Susanne and I were technically just friends and had been so for over a year. We had had a falling out and there were some unresolved things between us—mainly stemming from the fact that she was unhappy with her life and somehow wasn't necessarily able to deal when good things happened to me.

Also coming to the party was Emily, a gal I had dated briefly in the winter and spring of 2003—whatever "dating" meant when she lived in North Carolina and I lived in Berkeley and we saw each other maybe three times in four months. But, truth be told, she probably still carried a little torch for me. Emily had just moved to D.C. and didn't really know many people, so I was trying to be friendly by inviting her, too.

Susanne and I arrived at Kathryn's for the pre-party. After watching various guests arrive and after two glasses of wine, I saw Serena (a friend of a friend of Kathryn's). She was wearing high black boots, a black skirt, and a tanktop-style sweater in purple angora. But I didn't go over to talk to her.

Serena and Kathryn talked. Kathryn learned that Serena had gone to the University of North Carolina and had this particular scholarship there, the Morehead Scholarship. Kathryn told Serena she should meet me, since I had also gone to UNC and had that same scholarship. (This is a big coincidence—only about fifty people get the Morehead in any given year.)

So Serena and I were introduced. We ascertained that she had graduated three years ahead of me, which is why we didn't know each other in college. Because the majority of people who win this scholarship are North Carolina residents, I was curious if she was from North Carolina, like I am.

The people from outside of North Carolina who got this scholarship typically came from elite prep schools. So it was always a bit of a joke among the scholarship recipients that these elite kids got a full scholarship to a public university, which they probably didn't need from a financial standpoint. So I asked Serena if she was from North Carolina. She said no. I asked where she went to high school. She said, "Exeter." And—having just met this person perhaps three minutes ago—I said, "Oh, so you're one of those private-school Moreheads."

This is a tendency I have—to tease people I barely know. Two glasses of wine only exacerbated that tendency. Sometimes it works fine. The person laughs and teases me back, and we're on our way to a delightful repartee. The downside, of course, is that I run the risk of seeming boorish and offensive. Which is probably how I appeared to Serena. Unwittingly, I had stumbled upon a slightly sensitive subject. Among the Exeter student body, Serena had been far removed from the financial elite kids whose parents owned a yacht and summered in Monte Carlo or whatever. Oops.

However, and to her everlasting credit, Serena swallowed any indignation and changed the subject. She had noticed my watchband, mentioned it, the subject was changed, and we went on chatting.

At some point, we moved on to Saint Ex. About thirty or so people walked from the apartment, and of course there were more people at Saint Ex itself. So it was pretty much a loud crowded party. I ended up drinking maybe four gin and tonics in the first couple hours (as they were "free"). In other words, I was drunk. Susanne got really drunk very quickly. Notoriously prone to nausea, she barfed in the alley behind Saint Ex. I was there to "take care" of her. She ended up mostly passed out on a banquette. I kept finding excuses to touch Serena's very fuzzy, very soft angora sweater. I insisted that she touch my pants leg, since my pants had kind of a velvety texture themselves. This is what passes for flirting after I've had four mixed drinks.

Serena was exceedingly aware that I was "with" two other women. At some point she told a friend of Kathryn's, "Someone brought too many dates!" Around eleven-thirty, some of us went downstairs where there was a DJ. I was essentially

and . . .
action!

Which Hollywood pairing produced more than a film or TV show?

A. Ben Affleck & Jennifer Garner
B. Christopher & Dana Reeve
C. Julia Roberts & Danny Moder
D. Matt Damon & Luciana Bozán Barroso
E. Will Smith & Jada Pinkett
F. Johnny Carson & Alexis Maas

Answer: A, C and E

A. Ben and Jen met on the set of *Pearl Harbor* in 2001 (Garner was married to actor Scott Foley at the time). They later worked together on *Daredevil* in 2003 (Garner was still married and Affleck was engaged to Jennifer Lopez). In '04 Garner and Foley and Affleck and Lopez split and Garner and Affleck got together. The two married in '05.

B. Superman met his Lois Lane at a cabaret at the Williamstown Theatre Festival in Massachusetts in the summer of 1987. Christopher was in the audience and introduced himself to Dana after the show.

C. The Pretty Woman met Danny Moder, a cinematographer and the man she says she was "born to love and be the wife of" on the set of *The Mexican* in 2000.

D. Damon chatted up his bartender in Miami in 2003. He was in town filming *Stuck on You*.

E. The two met in 1995 on the set of *The Fresh Prince of Bel-Air*. The story goes that Pinkett auditioned for the role of Smith's girl-friend, but didn't get it because she was so much shorter than he.

F. Alexis Maas walked by Johnny Carson's beachfront home with an empty wineglass. Johnny approached and offered her a refill. She became the late night host's fourth wife. At an earlier roast for Carson, funnyman Bob Newhart had joked, "Johnny's first wife was named Jody. His second was JoAnne, and now he's married to Joanna . . . the man just won't go for new towels." With Alexis, it looks like he finally had to.

dancing with Susanne, Emily, and Serena simultaneously. Serena was also sort of watching this other guy—essentially writing me off because she assumed that I must be with one of these other women. At midnight on the dance floor, I kissed Emily, then Susanne, then Serena. Except I really *kissed* Serena. Chalk up that bit of forwardness to the liquor and the angora sweater.

I think it was at this point that Serena realized, "Hey, maybe he's not with one of those other women." Obviously, on that New Year's Eve neither of us had an inkling that we were "meant" to be together. But we committed to seeing what would happen. After only several days of talking on the phone, Serena said that we should spend time together. It wasn't worth the long-distance bill if things weren't going to work in person. So I traveled to D.C. for the Martin Luther King Day holiday weekend.

Even then we weren't head-over-heels in love, but we kept at it. Serena came to Austin a few weeks after that. After that second meeting, when I traveled to D.C. and we spent the weekend together, Serena summed up our time together as, "Well, I didn't fall madly in love, but I didn't want to be by myself, either." I tease her about how qualified that statement sounds, but in all honesty that's how I felt too.

advice for others
take a risk.

Maybe this all boils down to nothing more than "take a risk." Or that love is something that you have to work to discover, not something that happens to you. I guess we think of this as valuable advice when people we know seem unwilling to entertain the prospect of an inconvenient romance (like New Yorkers who can't date anyone who doesn't live in Manhattan).

I think our story also speaks to those who seem to want overwhelming evidence of a major connection before they'll proceed. As such, maybe they either want less work or less risk. So I guess the lesson we drew from this is: Decide together to give something a chance, even when it always requires an annoying non-direct flight through the Dallas or Houston airports and, more importantly, when you don't really know what will happen, or whether the effort will pay dividends.

how jill
met jim

Met: February 1997 in Washington, D.C. Jill was twenty-three and Jim was twenty-one.

Married: June 2003

I was planning a ladies' night at a local bar called Madame's Organ. I tried to call the place to see what kind of music they were playing that night and they didn't answer the phone. If they had answered the phone, I never would have gone. They were playing bluegrass and I, being from Staten Island, was a disco girl.

I got there early, both my friends were late, and there was that bluegrass band. I decided to wait at the bar. While I was waiting, I saw a guy with a cool dark-brown leather jacket with a 70s butterfly collar come in. He had beautiful long hair just kind of whishing around—I only saw the back of his head—and I thought, "I want to meet him!"

I saw him go upstairs when one of my friends showed up. When I saw the guy, I told myself, "I'm not going to talk to him first." I had been meeting different guys recently and feeling like they wouldn't always call back. I thought, "Maybe I'm being too aggressive—I'll just let the guys come to me."

I mentioned to my friend that we should check upstairs for our other friend, maybe she had come in already, and all of a sudden I heard a voice behind me. Someone said, "Don't go upstairs, it sucks upstairs." I turned around and saw that it was him, with his hair now in a ponytail. I thought, "Well, in that case, he talked to me first!" But by that point, he had turned back around. I tugged on his ponytail and when he turned around I said, "I like your jacket." His reply was, "Salvation Army."

We started talking, and I learned that he and his friends had all come to see the bluegrass band. He hadn't been out in months, so his friends dragged him out that night and they specifically came to hear the music. By the end of the night, my other friend had finally come in. She asked, "Who are these guys you're talking to?" Some of them were wearing overalls (but not Jim, who was wearing a cool outfit). By the end of the night I was dancing in front of the stage with his friends and having a great time.

At the end of the night, when he was leaving, Jim took out his Palm Pilot. He said, "Give me your number, I'll plug it in." And I said, "No," and he said, "No, no, I've got this little machine here and I'll put it in." Again, I said, "No." He didn't understand. He looked up and said, "Why?" I said, "Are you going to wait to call me? I'll take your number and then I'll call you." He said, "Are you going to make me wait?" I thought, "Well, I guess not now!" He'd know I'd be waiting on purpose.

I called him the next day. I never *ever* do that, that's the cardinal sin. We had our first real date at Kramerbooks. I thought to myself, "Well, it's a bar, a bookstore, and a café. This is one of the tests. If he's in the bookstore reading a book and not at the bar, he's a good guy." So I came in and he was reading a book on quantum physics!

advice for others
get out of the house.

Go out often. Join clubs and social groups, and hit the bars, bookstores, and parks. Don't expect to meet Mr. or Ms. Right immediately. Have fun and live your life; desperation shows.

how john *& * daisy *met*

Met: October 2004 in Urbana, Ohio. Both John and Daisy were sixty-two.
Married: Valentine's Day 2006

John: After my wife Katherine died, my cousin insisted I go to a grief support group. I found a group in Urbana that was close to where I lived. It was a six-week session, and I learned a lot.

I didn't realize what you go through feelings-wise and I felt it was very helpful. My wife-to-be, Daisy, was in that group.

Daisy: After the support group was over in October 2005, the group decided to have get-togethers so we wouldn't lose touch. I hosted a dinner at my house in January. We met again, John and I, and after that he mentioned a restaurant in Springfield. I had gone and—help me with the story, John.

John: She had gone and said it was very good. I said that on the nights I taught, I stopped there rather than cook and asked if she wanted to join me, which she did. At one of the dinners I told her a friend was moving and we used to go bicycling. I asked if she bicycled and she said she hadn't since her husband died.

Daisy: So we started bicycling together. Then there was a second support group. And I'll let you tell it—

John: A couple of women had asked me to go, but I have a fairly busy schedule. They called me a couple of times because the moderator wanted someone who had lost someone six months prior to show that life goes on and it's important that life goes on. So I went. A Baptist minister ran it at the funeral home. It was the old governor's mansion, by the way; a beautiful old house with upstairs meeting rooms and a funeral home downstairs. So it was basically a funeral home—

Daisy: He forgot to tell you I wasn't in that group of women that called him!

[Both laugh.]

John: We did start bicycling and we were bicycling quite a bit—it seemed to increase [*both laugh*] and we got to know each other better. Daisy had purchased a patio swing, and after rides we'd sit on the patio and swing on the swing and get to know each other better.

Daisy: It was a friendship thing. And then one day after bicycling, we were resting in the grass and we sat back-to-back and that was the first time I really felt there might be something there. Carry on, John—

John: I really felt I was falling for her. I hadn't dated anyone for forty years, as I'd been married. Daisy had been married for forty-one years. We both had families—I have three daughters, she has two sons. We had good marriages. I knew the feeling, but I wasn't quite sure where to go from there. So I called my youngest daughter and told her to get her husband on the phone and—they knew Daisy, knew who she was—and I said, 'I think I'm falling in love with her.' And my daughter said, 'Does she feel the same way?' I said I didn't know and she said,

quote/ unquote	"He makes me slow down and eat lunch, which I used not to do. We have different philosophies. I've been so disciplined. His process is 'Chill, don't kill yourself.'" —Jennifer Lopez, about husband Marc Anthony

'Dad! You have to ask her or you're going to get hurt.' I called Daisy right after. I asked if I could come over and she said yes. She was puzzled—it was later than usual. We were on the swing. Usually I'm a talker and she said, 'I'll give you a nickel for your thoughts—'

Daisy: A penny.

John: A penny. And then she said, 'I'm sorry, I shouldn't try to find out what you're thinking.' And I said, 'You should. I'm trying to think how to ask you if you love me.'

Daisy: He said something like, 'I love you and do you love me?' I was in total shock.

John: She said she answered right away, but it felt like an hour to me! [Both laugh.] Daisy pitches horseshoes. I had gone a couple of times to watch her. She pitches about 48 percent ringers. She was going out to the world championships in Wyoming and she said, 'I'd like you to go with me.' I said, 'On one condition: I want to go as husband and wife.' I'm Catholic. Under special circumstances you are allowed to get married someplace other than in a Catholic church and by other than a Catholic priest. My pastor agreed it was special circumstances. One day we told the reverend who ran the grief support group that we wanted to talk to him after the meeting, and he said 'Sure, fine.' We said, 'The final meeting is Valentine's Day and we'd like to cater the dinner rather than pitch in.' He said, 'You don't have to do something like that' and I said, 'I haven't finished. We want to get married.'

Daisy: We felt the grief support group was like family. We had the wedding catered, had a harpist, and a flutist, and friends who sang.

John: We have had such great times together. It's unbelievable. I am the luckiest guy in the world—I have fallen in love with two wonderful women. When we got engaged, Daisy didn't want an engagement ring. I said, 'Why not?' Why didn't you?

Daisy: I never wanted one. But I have one now and it sparkles so nicely.

John: I had the diamond from my first wife's ring mounted on Daisy's ring.

Daisy: He said, 'How would you feel about having the diamond I gave Kathy?' I think it was an honor he wanted me to have it. [*She cries.*]

John: We feel blessed. Even before we got really serious, we could talk about each other's spouses and it wasn't a hindrance like some people say it is.

Daisy: We delayed our honeymoon to take it during the world championships. But something was wrong. By the time we got to Colorado to visit grandkids along the way, he was in so much pain. The doctors kept him in the ICU for four days. Needless to say, we canceled the horseshoe trip.

John: Now people say, 'They got married in a funeral home and spent their honeymoon in a hospital!'

Daisy: We hated to quit going to the support group but I said, 'We're not grieving anymore.'

advice for others
life goes on.

We both realized that if you have a successful marriage, remarrying is a compliment to the spouse who's deceased.